Soul Evolution:

Past Lives and Karmic Ties

A Lightworker's Guidebook

Tina Erwin
Laura Van Tyne

Soul Evolution
Past Lives and Karmic Ties

Copyright © 2017
Tina Erwin and Laura Van Tyne
Published by Crystal Pointe Media Inc.

ISBN-13: 978- 1732267398
ISBN-10: 1732267391

DISCLAIMER
The contents of this publication are intended for educational and informative use only.
They are not to be considered directive nor as a guide to self-diagnosis or self-treatment. Before embarking on any therapeutic regimen, it is absolutely essential that you consult with and
obtain the approval of your personal physician or health care provider.

Cover Design by Laura Van Tyne

Other Works

Books
- The Lightworker's Guide to Healing Grief
- The Lightworker's Guide to Everyday Karma
- Ghost Stories from the Ghosts' Point of View, Trilogy
- Karma and Frequency

Podcast
- The Karmic Path Podcast: Available anywhere you listen to podcasts

Knowledge Library
- On-Demand Spiritual and Metaphysical Classes found at www.TheKarmicPath.com

Table of Contents

Karma Never Wastes Energy: How We Met

My husband and I were exhausted.

There were months of sleepless nights. Months of hearing a tiny pair of terrorized feet racing down the hall, leaping at the speed of light into our bed. There were months of me falling asleep in our daughter's bedroom so that my husband could get a halfway decent night's sleep to enable him to function at work the next morning. I spent hours praying for guidance on how to help our 6-year-old daughter and our entire family, praying for the safety and well-being of my family's soul. I also spent hours praying for an answer and some form of respite from the hell that had pervaded our household. We were living in the darkness of an extremely haunted house, a house that felt oppressive and sooty all the time. Somehow our home had become what I would call a "Ghost Super Highway." There's this thing about ghosts: they don't need to sleep!

One ghost in particular caused me deep concern: Annabelle. It was as if the light had gone out of our lives when this ghost, this terrifying ghost child, came to live with us. What do you do with such a situation? How can a child be terrifying? Why is it so hard to cross over a ghost? *Why don't people know how to do this?*

I searched for psychic/spiritual help for eighteen of the longest, most torturous months I could recall. Along the way there was one tiny glimmer of hope. I was told by one of the psychics I met that while she was not the right person for me that I would, eventually "meet a woman in uniform." However, in my exhaustion and desperation, that glimmer of hope was forgotten and lost for over a year.

I never gave up. I contacted countless psychics and

religious organizations, seeking help for our predicament. Nothing worked. Nothing felt right. The one true thing I knew was that I needed to trust my intuition. During this entire 18-month search I kept hearing this little voice in my head saying, "You have one chance to get this right. You have one chance to find the right person."

And honestly, I had no idea what that meant at the time. My frustration was mounting. I have a Master's Degree in Education, but nothing in my career prepared me for this.

Very few people knew the hell my family was living. Mostly because, well, who would believe all that was happening to us? But my sister-in-law knew: she knew about our "fourth daughter, Annabelle." Late one afternoon, she called me to tell me her friend, Sue, had met someone who might be able to help us. At this point, I had little hope, and less left to lose, so I called her.

"May I speak to Tina Erwin, please?"

A rather cheerful voice responded. I was so exhausted that I detested cheerfulness at that time and yet I had to tell her enough to see if she could help us.

"Your number was given to me by a woman named Sue whom you met recently, I believe? Um, I have a living, psychic child and we have a ghost child named Annabelle living with us. She's been with us for what seems like forever now. My daughter and the ghost started out as 'friends' but then the ghostly Annabelle decided she wanted me to be her mom and she wants my daughter out of the picture. Annabelle now stabs, kicks and hurts my daughter all the time. She teases and torments her day and night then tells her horrible things to get a reaction out of her."

I found myself pouring out our story like a river of woe. Tina listened patiently.

"We have been searching for help and no one seems to be able to help us. There have been a few psychics who claimed to have 'gotten rid of her.' But she always returns. We even went to a high mass in Annabelle's name. The church council told my daughters and I, that Annabelle was now in the arms of God. But Annabelle just laughed at those people and turned around and hopped in the car with us and I took her back home. Is this something you can help me with?"

"Yes, of course," She responded.

And I remember thinking to myself, "That's what all the other well-meaning psychics and religious institutions said." As it turned out, this time was different: this time it worked! Tina helped me to cross Annabelle over into what Tina called The Heaven World.

Karma must have put me in this position because I needed those experiences of learning what was true and not true in this paranormal realm. As it turns out, practicing due diligence becomes paramount in the unseen world. I learned what to do and what not to do. I also had to ramp up my own psychic abilities which had been lying dormant since I was a child.

Those 18 months were torturous and exhausting. I also know that had I met Tina at the beginning of this journey, I would not have been able to appreciate all the lessons learned along the way, how her methodologies truly work and that they are of the highest spiritual service.

Had we met earlier, she would not have needed my services. We would not have become business partners, and more importantly, friends. It turns out that one psychic was right: I did meet a woman in uniform, a Commander's uniform. Tina is a retired Naval Officer. As it turned out, she needed help getting her books published and marketed, thus a natural partnership was born.

Since we met, we have published many books together. (My story is one of the first stories in _Ghost Stories_ *from the Ghosts' Point of View, Vol. 1)*, and we began the podcast *The Karmic Path*. We are excited to share the spiritual truths that can bring peace and joy to both the living and the dead.

Our karmic paths are now joined. The books that we put out are designed to help anyone on their spiritual/karmic path to understand a bit more about how the world of the Divine and Earthly existence blend together in our daily lives.

Tina and I are just beginning to understand the significance of the work that we can perform as we walk this karmic path of spiritual service together.

Laura Van Tyne

Acknowledgements

We all collect people on our karmic paths and some of them can be a tremendous asset along the way. This is especially true for the both of us. We enjoy and have learned so much from everyone we have met and will meet.

Tina's brother Pierre Debs was instrumental in helping to educate us in the often - mysterious ways of karma. Her brother Paul Debs has been a loyal supporter, challenging the both of us with probing questions and poignant examples of karma in action. These two men have been instrumental in helping us all along the way, on our karmic paths.

We are also very grateful to our husbands, Troy Erwin and Sean Van Tyne; it is not always easy living with us because we never know what the next phone call or email will bring. They have been ever supportive.

Thank you to Amee Erwin for her work in helping us to get this published.

We are grateful to all of our friends who have attended the many evenings we have offered to discuss the nuances of metaphysics. We called the group Light Times because we wanted to keep the energy fun, filled with enlightenment and insight. Our heartfelt thanks go out to all of these lovely people who came to share my path.

And finally, our deepest gratitude to Dr. Ibrahim Karim for the knowledge of Biogeometry® he has shared with us. We are thrilled and honored to have his words grace the foreword of this book.

And thank you to all who read these books and begin to look at the world in a different way. May you walk with the angels along your karmic path.

Tina Erwin, CDR, USN, (Ret) and Laura Van Tyne

Foreword

The soul is probably one of the most discussed topics in literature, since every civilization in history seeks to explain soul evolution in its own way. There are countless interpretations of soul-related topics like reincarnation, the afterlife, karma, creation, soul mates, purgatory, heaven, hell, sin, mind, Divinity and God, that it can become bewildering.

People brought up in a closed culture or religion usually believe in their own interpretation of how a soul evolves, and discard all others in a judgmental way, leading to all kinds of controversies as well as inner and outer emotional conflicts.

In our modern times, the ease of travel all over the world plus the abundance of information through the media has slowly eroded the boundaries separating global cultures.

People are moving out of their protective cultural cocoons into a diversity of worldviews that in many ways, shakes their old spiritual foundations. Often, they follow another more attractive culture's doctrine because it has an exotic nature giving it a certain social appeal.

So, if you are seeking a modern interpretation of soul evolution, one that will help you to see the balance between the invisible and the visible reality, this book will help to guide your way.

Ultimately, this may enable you to see your own belief system differently. See it not the way you have been taught but in a new way through the guidance of your heart which will enable you to embrace all other doctrines. This will provide an inner richness to your understanding that is not found by leaving one system for another.

Spiritual studies of soul evolution bring you to the conclusion, that only when your heart is activated will you find that the resulting inner ethical values become your guidance. These are universal values that will embrace and apply to all beliefs and cultures because they act on the essence of things. This focus on Soul Evolution as written within these pages is on ethics and the free will option of personal responsibility, not merely on the outward manifestations of right and wrong that produce the destructive elements of guilt and inner conflicts.

I personally find that the authors of this book have dealt with the topic of soul evolution in a very effective and simple-to-understand process. It is also in a way that feels right for the heart. This activation of the heart through involving our more emotional right-brain mode of perception is what will take us over the bridge of insight and understanding. Then the seeker will be able to savour the universal truths that are not accessible to the "left-brain only" mode of sensory perception.

The authors of this book have studied BioGeometry® and the Physics of Quality. These concepts of the multidimensional aspects of Pythagorean Harmonics are based on the ancient sciences of vibration founded in the teachings of Ancient Egypt.

These concepts of Harmonics, or frequency, are the laws of resonance. Think of the tonal quality of musical strings. Each string sounds a different note or tone, based on the length of that string and its vibration. However, when we are speaking of soul evolution, we are each striking a cord, or tone based on the "tonal quality" of our current level of soul evolution. The possibilities for string lengths range from zero to infinity. The concept of this massive range of notes, or resonance of our souls, symbolically spans everything in the invisible absolute reality beyond our three-dimensional world, beyond our perceived physical dimension. What this means is that as souls evolve, they begin to resonate with higher and higher "tone levels" until they reach the level of the "music of the spheres" or the higher dimensional levels of the spiritual planes. This is the Law of Universal Multidimensional Resonance.

The Law of Universal Multidimensional Resonance manifests across the board of "spiritual soul strings" from zero to infinity. This is the way we access information through qualitative interaction on all dimensions, both visible and invisible.

This might seem a bit complex, but it is actually a very practical way of accessing and working with multidimensional energy quality. And multidimensional energy quality is something as humble as observing a flower and then sensing the flower in its surroundings, sensing the purpose of the flower, the color and how the color of the flower fits into life itself. You tap in to the many dimensions/multidimensional elements or energy quality of the flower. And this can be on any level such as life force, emotional, mental and ultimately, on the spiritual dimensions.

The authors have correctly identified the dimension where the soul dwells and the domain of karma, reincarnation and related subjects as beyond the time-space boundaries of our electromagnetic universe governed by the speed of light. In other words, the authors are offering the means by which we can understand how our soul evolves to return to the Divine by our spiritual growth, which is measured by the physics of the quality of our frequency. When situations are outside the constraints of our physical sensory mode of perception where we have no cause and effect, things cannot be comprehended by the mind. In this situation how can we understand the true nature of such topics that are beyond our physical reality? Perhaps it is with books just such as this one.

A very important point arises here: How can we

evaluate the different versions of translations or interpretations of how a soul evolves? First, we choose the one in our language and nearest to our culture and then, eventually, we evaluate the information through our own gut feeling. The more we feel at ease with these concepts, the more it is a correct interpretation of what we believe constitutes absolute reality. Eventually, these personal ideas will be projected into the afterlife makeup of what we believe to be true.

It is therefore at the end for authors like Tina Erwin and Laura Van Tyne to produce a logical, founded-in-recognizable-reality, or left-brain intellectual model. This flexible model also has an emotional bond to our right brain and heart. The duality of the balance between right and left-brains, enables these authors to connect the reader to the universality of absolute reality or the Divine. It is like a musical note becoming self-aware of its role in the omnipresent universal symphony of creation.
Dr. Ibrahim Karim, Ph.D. D.Sc.

Dr. Ibrahim Karim is the founder of the Science of BioGeometry® started in the early 1970s. BioGeometry® is the science that uses shapes, colors, motion and sound to induce harmony into the subtle energy qualities of the environment. At the core of this harmony is a subtle energy quality found in the transcendental centers of the forming process of nature and is the main quality in sacred power spots of humanity that give a spiritual dimension to the timeless monuments erected since the dawn of humanity. With his experience as an architect and a scientist, Dr. Karim has synergized aspects of Pythagorean Harmonics, Subtle energy sciences, Radiesthesia, Geobiology, Building Biology, Sacred Architecture, and modern wave theories to produce a new Physics of Quality from which the science of BioGeometry® emerged.

How Can We Be So Different?

I remember as a child wondering about the "hows" and "whys" when it came to certain people who were in my life. In middle school I had a teacher who was simply a jerk to all the students. This teacher thrived on humiliating others. I was 12 and I remember thinking, "How on earth did this person even get a teaching job?" Looking back, perhaps this teacher really taught us much more than the subject matter. Maybe those students and parents needed the experience as a part of their soul evolution. Perhaps this cruel teacher was more of a karmic teacher than most realized. Could it be that this educator gave parents and students the opportunity to stand up for what was right? Or is it possible that we were placed as students to teach this teacher what kindness and compassion were? At the end of it all, there are a lot of "maybes." Perhaps if we start looking at difficult situations with a karmic eye, we can start to look for the subtle lessons that can teach us more than we could ever imagine.

I have three daughters who have all grown up in the same house with my husband and me as their parents. Yet I have often marveled at how each child could be so different. One daughter is a scientist, with a degree in biology and chemistry. Another is studying to be a special education teacher. Our youngest daughter is exceptionally psychic and has a deep passion for animals and nature.

We are spiritual beings having a human experience. It is not the other way around. If we look at this concept, we can learn to see a much larger picture of our soul evolution. What roles do our souls' compiled history play in shaping our evolutionary path? If we look at the history of this planet, there is no country, culture or group of people that is immune to abuse. Abuse has been a prominent theme of this planet for millennia. How do we change that? Can it be fixed? What roles do our souls' compiled history play in shaping our evolutionary path? Since we all have lived many lives and those lives are experiences that we needed for our soul evolution, how does this play into our personalities and how does

this affect our karma? These questions prompted Tina and me to offer our perspective on these age-old questions.
Laura Van Tyne

I am the eldest of four children: four very distinct personalities with different hopes and dreams. Two of us were/are driven with clear missions in front of us and two of us saw life differently. Our individual views of how we should be living were right for each of us. We loved each other as siblings, but we did not always understand what motivated the other brother or sister.

I remembered wondering, from the time I was a child, how we could possibly be this different if we all came from the same parents? This became part of my own life mission to figure out. So, when I was twelve, I started studying astrology and realized that our family was comprised of six different astrological signs, as described by Linda Goodman in her book Sun Signs. We were all over the astrological wheel: Pisces, Gemini, Leo, Virgo, Libra and Scorpio. That explained quite a bit, but I realized that this could not be all of it; there had to be more. I also wanted to know where we were before we were born. What happens when we die? Is there more than just living and dying?

I had no idea that by asking these questions I was embarking on my own karmic path of spiritual advancement. I worked diligently to collect the following concepts that rang true for me deep within my core being.

Christ talked about life everlasting. He never discussed death everlasting. I found it comforting to know I wouldn't become compost, but that who I was, what I had done would not be lost, wasted or forgotten. But I still wanted to know where and how this process worked and I realized that it didn't make sense to me without embracing reincarnation.

I realized that Christ did not die on the cross for my sins. I embraced the concept that this dynamic being died in this manner to positively manipulate karma on the planet, a powerful and astounding concept that filled me with gratitude. This made sense to me. He did not die for sins I had yet to commit: a concept that felt inherently illogical.

I learned that we are all spiritual beings having a human experience, and that we spend more time in the other realms than we do in a mortal body.

We are all supposed to be evolving to higher and higher levels of spiritual advancement.

We come back, life after life, to improve our standing in this mortal classroom on this beautiful planet.

We get life, after life, after life, to learn, grow, offer spiritual service and develop within ourselves increasingly sophisticated levels of compassion and wisdom.

The karma we earn in each life is returned to us in the next life and sometimes in the life we are currently living.

Free Will is the greatest and most powerful gift from God to empower our spiritual advancement if we use it wisely.

There is no learning in perfection: to advance we have to have both positive and negative experiences that will earn us wisdom for future lives.

Who we are, and who we have been, never dies. We never stop being ourselves both in life and in death.

Over time, with consistent study and a burning desire to really understand this, I realized that we are who we are based on the following powerful factors that look something like the graphic below. Based on that concept that there are powerful factors, I have been able to begin to define in a most humble way what may comprise a soul.

Tina Erwin

What is Soul Evolution?

Our souls are comprised of many elements that shape who we are. This book discusses those elements and how they impact our soul's growth. These elements include:

- Karma
- Past Lives
- Soul Frequency
- Free Will Choices
- Soul Purpose/Mission
- Soul Evolution Status
- Current Life Experiences
- Early Childhood Experiences

Do All Souls Evolve?

Soul Evolution means that we are all spiritual beings using our human experiences to evolve to higher and higher divine levels.

The purpose of that human experience is to offer us

theme and variation in the exercise of free will choices. Did we learn from each life lesson offered? If so, then theoretically, we can all progress to higher and higher spiritual levels through the acquisition of experiences, the give and take of daily life and embracing the humility of great wisdom. When we have acquired a predetermined level of wisdom and spiritual growth, we stop reincarnating on this planet. We "graduate" to live in the Higher Realms of the fifth dimension or the Heaven World. That sounds pretty straightforward.

But Soul Evolution is not a straight shot. We don't merely enroll in the "first grade" of spiritual school and automatically get promoted to the next higher level on some predetermined pathway. There is no place to apply to attend Spiritual University either, because Free Will is a powerful element that can take our spiritual pathway in a tremendous variety of directions. Free Will is the fascinating variable in the wheel of eternal life.

That concept sounded easy enough: Free Will, you get to do what you want – right?

But nothing in the misty land of anyone's spiritual path is that straightforward or that simple. How long does it take to evolve out of the reincarnation cycle?

It is important to understand the "timeframe" of Soul Evolution. First of all, time only exists on Earth. Time does not exist in the other dimensions because it is unnecessary. This means that we have eternity to work on our spiritual path.

Earth is such a perfectly powerful and plentiful schoolhouse because it offers us the **time** *to experience life, and the* **space** *in which to give meaning to that life.* But time and space cannot exist without **gravity**. Earth is the ideal location because it can provide time, space and gravity, the magic trio to offer the precise setting for all the characters in the story of our lives to act out their roles, life after life. But we don't have a script.

We have Free Will in how we will respond to each page of experiences, encounters, traumas and joys presented to us over eons of Earth time. Each Free Will decision we make determines the next step on our path but it is never so easy as simply putting one foot in front of another.

Life, that glorious challenge throws other all kinds of unimaginable monkey wrenches in the seemingly smoothly flowing gears on our path. Life is what happens to us while we are making other plans. How we handle those "other plans" creates karma and we karmically create what our next experiential opportunities will be, whether we are aware of the concept of karma or not. Each decision can elevate us, take us sideways or cause us to regress.

Each lifetime can offer numerous karmic lessons but for our purpose, let us focus on just one type of example: Power over others.

Power can take the form of a parent's power over a child, a boss's power over an employee, a criminal's power over a victim or the power of life and death. Power over anyone in any situation is something with which we can all identify.

The lesson to be learned is all about the power one person has over another and the right use of power.

Let us say that in this life something terrible happens to you, physical or sexual abuse, or even spiritual abuse. Whoever did these things to you seems like the bad guy. You learn abuse of power from this person and so you abuse someone else because, well, isn't that how you are supposed to do things – the way things were done to you?

Here is the karmic lesson: you really hated what was done to you, yet you now do this, but your life isn't any better. The more people abuse you, the madder you get, and the more you abuse until finally, one day, karma collapses and you either end up profoundly depressed, commit a terrible crime or die an angry, bitter person.

What is the lesson? Let us say that you were physically and/or sexually abused. You are hurt and angry. You are faced with a choice. Do you now abuse other people? Do you stay a victim? Or do you decide to face the pain, *embrace the experience* and *heal?* Your abusers are your most profound teachers. Remove yourself from the emotion and look at the lesson. If you hear yourself saying that you just can't do that, then get someone to help you: find a teacher to help you embrace the lesson.

Your abusers were themselves abused. If you continue to be either an abuser or victim, then the pattern continues for the next thousand years or more. Imagine the tremendous power of changing a pattern for the positive for the next thousand years!

Let's say that your abuser dies, whew! Great to be off the hook! But wait there will always be someone to take his place. Karma is so fair and just that it never releases us without giving us the opportunity to fully learn to face our tormentors emotionally, to face that fear, to learn to heal and to love those who have hurt us.

Look at it this way: before your abuser came into this life, someone gave them a script too and part of their job was to learn the lesson of abuse. Since they did not learn that lesson that means that they continued to abuse. The spiritually evolving soul will see the power of the experience, even the negative ones and will use this experience as the path to healing. This is the path to forgiveness: they gave you an opportunity. Now choose to use it. The beauty of karma is that we are always offered choices. The more we are conscious of our choices, the more we can heal. Karma is always fair and just. Learning the lesson will bring great peace.

Basically, this is Karmic law: karma keeps presenting

the lesson until you really, truly get it. Karma will test you to see if the answer lives within you. When the truth, when the answer finally lives within you, then that awful lesson is no longer needed. When the lesson is no longer needed, those terrible things cease happening to you and you can heal. This life and the next will be quantitatively better. This is soul evolution. That which is not learned in this life is carried forward into the next life to learn.

Can Souls De-Evolve?

It would be wonderful to say that all souls progress, and evolve equally at a prescribed, divinely preordained pace, but this is untrue. We know, from our own encounters, that some people are cruel and vicious. Others steal, lifting the levels of greed they can achieve to new heights.

Some souls play power games and rob those around them of their sense of self-worth, the bullies of the world.

Each soul is making choices on his or her spiritual/karmic path that are retarding spiritual growth. One may have powerful experiences but those events are not helping to elevate his or her soul. But karma never wastes energy, and the experiences that this negative person provides for those around them can be powerful karmic opportunities to stand up to the darkness or to allow themselves to be harmed by this person's negative energy.

Murderers are on a path of spiritual regression. But if we are all on a spiritual path, how can some regress in their soul evolution? Is this a karmic issue? How does this path of devolution begin?

Murder by serial killers, mass murders, or mass murder ordered by individual governments are all committed by persons on a spiritual path, but it is a dark path, one that makes that sooty, delusional soul think he or she has power but the truth is chillingly different. This soul is sinking farther and farther away from the light of the divine. How does any soul begin their descent along this sinister downward spiral?

It's quite simple really. It starts with one disgusting and tragically common event: sexual abuse.

The sexual center, or root charka, is among the most important power centers of the mortal body. This reproductive tract is part of the process of creation, especially when two people come together in marriage and love to create children. It takes power to create a new mortal being, to host a soul in a body and then deliver the child into life. The challenge is that this center is attractive to those who would steal this power from others, taking the innocence of childhood and the power potential that exists there. This is why someone who has been the victim of child sexual abuse or even an adult who has been raped (both male and female) feel robbed of something so exquisite in its preciousness that that person never feels the same again.

Many cancers begin in the reproductive tract because the person feels forever "soiled" by the invasive experience. This is challenging to heal both physically and emotionally.

Making matters worse, this terrible experience retards this soul's spiritual growth because the violation of trust, especially from an early age, has a profoundly negative effect on the person's personality and their perception of the world. It is as if a shadow self is with them now, something they would love to shed but cannot, no matter what they do. Time can help mitigate the trauma of the event, but it is as if the person is suffering from a chronic low level of post-traumatic stress disorder.

As bad as this situation is, the soul *still has free will* in how he or she will approach the world. <u>This is the crux of the matter.</u> This is a horrible experience. How will the soul deal with this experience as each moment of the rest of his or her life moves forward?

One woman was gang raped by her brothers for ten years. Her trauma was so severe that she was unable to ever have a meaningful relationship and, in fact, developed characteristics of a borderline personality disorder, meaning that she became so needy that she exhausted her friends. However, she chose to try to lead as positive a life as she possibly could.

A young man's abuse by his mother and stepfathers included sexual assault, constant beatings, verbal abuse and virtual imprisonment. Yet, despite this, he educated himself, became a wealthy businessman and tried to be a loving father to his children by his three marriages. However, he was completely unable to develop any deeply satisfying relationships. Something was always missing inside him; there was hollowness within him, as if he was unlovable. Yet he *never, ever physically hurt any of his children or his wives.* He never furthered the cycle of abuse. His free will choice helped him achieve a step up on his spiritual path despite his horrific childhood.

But other people do not choose so wisely. Some who are abused go on to abuse their wives and children. Some women who were beaten go on to murder their own children. When you look at them, it is as if they are not fully there, as if there is something so dead inside of them that they cannot remember whom they ever were.

There is a theory that some people are abused life after life and that each life the sexual, physical, emotional and/or spiritual abuse becomes increasingly worse. Why would this happen like this? Is this part of some sinister plan? What happens when these people die? Where do they go? Who is waiting for them and why? Does anyone help them?

Soul Drama at Death

Many people assume that when someone dies, that this is the end of things. They hope the person sought the light and moved on to Heaven. They "trust" that somehow their loved one is "alright" whatever that may mean. But life after death is so much more complicated than this, especially for someone who suffered abuse and/or severe trauma.

There is a spiritual component to everything we do both in life and death. All the events that shaped us in life, determine our frequency in death. The big question now is: what happens spiritually after death, when someone was abused in life? There is a theory that sexual abuse is an initiation into the dark side of the spiritual path because once this abuse takes place, a 4th dimension "controller" is now tied to this person, and for many thousands of years, tries to slowly but surely to take over the person's soul. This concept may be hard for some to fathom, so let's build the case.

Someone suffers terrible abuse. It is possible that the degree of abuse could be karmic, meaning that if the person did not do things in a previous life to overcome their initial abuse and seek the higher road, then in the next life, their abuse could be more severe. The reason for this is that sexual abuse damages the soul, creating the "Swiss cheese" effect meaning that the auric structure or force field around the soul is now full of holes from each moment/event of abuse. These holes in the force field, or auric field for the soul in a mortal body allow detrimental things to enter, from diseases and parasites, to bullying events and low self-esteem.

Seeking help for depression, or the darkness that envelopes the person often means that drugs are prescribed and initially these may help, but long term use only treats a symptom and does not address the underlying cause. Drugs also further enlarge the holes in the person's auric field. It's a tough cycle to break.

This vulnerability can create chronic problems unless the person seeks psychological *and* spiritual help. It is not enough to seek psychotherapy to help to heal the traumas of the initial and/or prolonged abuse. The person must also seek to heal along his or her spiritual path, recognizing that *there is no healing without incorporating God's help in the process.* This is not about making the person go to church. This is not about religion. It is about rediscovering the light inside you, that creative spark that initially connected you to God. You will not necessarily find it in a building of wood and stone. Each person's path of discovery is unique and they find that spark wherever it works for them.

If the person does not seek this help, then something else may occur. The sexually abused person may now feel as if he or she is a "puppet on a string," controlled by a dark being on another realm. If we believe that those who are dedicated to their spiritual path have Guardian Angels, would it not make sense that the converse is also true? Serial killers do not have Guardian Angels: they have Lower Astral Beings or Black Magicians, "Dark Lords," who control them – or try to control them as their mortal slaves. They use the toxic energy of the person's abuse as their sustenance. They are forever trying to corrupt people to be their constant energy sources. The energy of children is the purest, and the taking of a child's sexual energy is the most hideous form of spiritual theft. The people who steal this energy were themselves once innocent but they chose a darker path and now, as mortal people, they become the instigators of the abuse, as the puppets of darker beings in the 4th dimension.

These dark beings were once mortal people, who were initially corrupted, abused and traumatized life after life. They did nothing to find healing for this trauma and eventually they themselves graduated into the ranks of the darkest ones: they became drunk with evil power in the 4th dimension.

Black Magicians: Puppet Masters of the Lower Astral

Among the worst mortal perpetrators, or messengers, of these dark beings are priests, clergymen and cult leaders because they not only steal the person's sexual energy, they also deprive them spiritually of any connection to God. That cold isolation makes that person an easy target for these dark beings, these horrific puppeteers, manipulating human beings and torturing souls who die and end up in the 4th dimension. This is why the karma created by these mortal "men of god" or "men of the cloth" is far more intensely negative *because these men know the spiritual difference between right and wrong and they are using their free will to harm.* Even with a puppeteer, the person can still stop their own actions because mortal people still have free will – up to a point. Once enough of their soul has been affected by these dark beings, then, over time, they become soulless robots doing the bidding of the evil ones. But how does it work?

The abused soul, the "puppet on a string" has to decide how he or she will resist their controlling puppeteer for the rest of their life. Some people are so damaged that it is as if *a piece of their very soul is shaved off with the abuse received in each life.* If that person is unable to resist their handler, then in the next life, he or she has the potential to come back with a character disorder[1] and take more and more from those around them. When they die, more of their soul is shaved off. More of what

---

Character/Personality Disorders include but are not limited to: Paranoid, Schizoid, Schizotypal, Antisocial, Borderline, Histrionic, Narcissistic, Avoidant, Dependent, and Anankastic (obsessive-compulsive).

makes them human, compassionate, caring, loving, self-sacrificing and courageous is sliced off, life, after life, after life, after life, until eventually they reincarnate as a cold robotic killer. But it takes time and effort to get that soul to this level.

Puppeted souls progress through the various character disorders until they become a soul with multiple character or personality disorders, then on to a soul with mental health issues, like a paranoid schizophrenic and finally they are manipulated into reincarnating as a mass murderer, serial killer/sociopath or government perpetrator of mass murder.

This is how souls regress and devolve into the darkest realms of the lower astral, the 4th dimension. This shell of a soul can no longer remember who they were, what it felt like to be human or how to care about another living thing, human or animal: the energy of pain, torture and horror of their victims feeds their slave masters. These once mortal people have become soul food. What can now be done for these souls?

Cross any of these types of souls over into the Heaven World using *The Crossing Over Prayer*. Only then can this ghost's soul be restored. This person will never leave the Lower Astral until someone helps them to find the shattered pieces of their own soul identity. While he or she is alive, there is nothing that will restore that for them, no treatment, spiritual retreat or copious amounts of white light or sage will change a person/soul this far gone. Only God can help them *in the Heaven World*. Crossing them over then places the soul in the 5th dimension of light and love, from which to reincarnate instead of from the hideous reaches of the lower astral. Souls reincarnating from the lower astral often return in as few as five Earth-timed years. These are the children who exhibit violence at early ages and who terrify their families.

The time in the 5th dimension will necessitate healing, karmic balance, and insight. This can take sometimes hundreds of Earth-timed years, meaning that the soul may be gone from Earth for up to a thousand years. The person has to eventually repay the karma he or she created and reincarnate into a place commensurate with that karma. Reincarnating from the Heaven World means that the person should have more internal fortitude than they would have previously had. Karma will want to know if this person, once tempted, can resist the cruelties of their previous lives.

However, if a dastardly person dies without the benefit of crossing over into the Heaven World, the minions of the dark lords immediately meet them. These Lower Realm beings (the minions) then begin to torment the soul, taunting him or her, making sure that the suffering he or he may have received in life continues into death. This punishment continues until the soul agrees to become one of their puppets for the puppet masters as well. They learn how to feed on darkness, negativity, war, abuse, tragedy, sorrow, intense despair and self-hatred. These are the traits these dark magicians seek to eternally feed themselves. These are the traits of a soul with an extremely low soul frequency. There is only one thing that thwarts them, just one. A kind person assists the dead person by crossing him or her over into the Heaven World.

Placing every dark person into the Heaven World does not erase their karma; it merely stops the karma they are continuing to create in the 4th dimension. It also allows them an opportunity to own whatever is left of his or her original soul and begin the restoration process – and help them to remember who they used to be before so much of their soul was destroyed.

Karma Created from Past Lives

Returning to what comprises a soul, the next huge

element is the karma carried over from past lives. It is wise to remember that no one's karma is all good or bad. Karmic return on previous actions taken can appear in a wide range of opportunities. This is what a karmic do-over means. Karma determines so much about a person's life in theme and variation. There are two elements to the karma carried forward from previous lives.

The first one is the element of return on your karmic investment. How did you invest your energy and focus in each life? How would you like your life investment to be returned to you?

If you worked extremely hard perfecting some aspect of your life and it was positive, then in the next life you will be offered an even greater opportunity to continue to perfect that skill or ability. If you love math, you may be offered a more dynamic chance to use that ability for the highest good, but that is not the only element that can define a return on investment. Souls are not one-dimensional; they need an entire buffet of life experiences to fully develop and spiritually flower. But if you have spent your life ignoring the effect of your actions in one life, you may find yourself experiencing that same effect in the next life: an unhappy return on your investment.

So, using our mathematician example, suppose you were to desire to grow on even higher levels of spiritual advancement, *and offer those around you greater levels of spiritual growth and insight.* This karmic opportunity could be what happened in the remarkable book *Hidden Figures* by Margot Lee Shetterly and turned into a film by Theodore Melfi and Allison Schroeder. This true story traces the experiences of Katherine Johnson, a genius level mathematician and two of her fellow genius level female friends who were living in the Newport News, Virginia area of the United States. Mrs. Johnson was offered the karmic opportunity not only to be part of the

NASA mathematical/computer team who put the first men in space for Project Mercury and helped put the first man on the moon, but she also accepted the karma of doing this as a black woman in the 1960s. She changed the way genius-level men not only looked at women but *forced these men to develop a grudging respect for black women.* She and the other black women she worked with changed how NASA did business in a time of tremendous racial tension. Mrs. Johnson stepped up to her karmic opportunity and, in her own humble way, changed the world in which she lived in no small measure. This was not an easy path. It required courage and stamina; she had to believe in herself and develop a determination to see the job to completion. She has a building named after her at NASA, a motion picture about her life and the admiration of a grateful nation. She created tremendous karma in this life. One can only imagine the karmic opportunities that await her in the next life.

Let us look at another example. Perhaps in a past life, you were in charge of managing Native American territories, when settlers were moving west. In that life, you decided that you hated these "savages" because they looked differently from you and were creating problems for the European wagon trains. So, you organized raiding parties and massacred entire tribal enclaves. You showed no mercy to man, woman or child. What could you expect in a future life? Some people have speculated that many of those cavalrymen returned as Native Americans in these times, so that they could experience the many challenges that define life on a Tribal Reservation. If you used that life to learn and grow, then the process of atonement you were experiencing would further your progress on your spiritual path. If, however, you became a depressed alcoholic, became abusive and represented the worst of your tribe, what karma might you expect in a future life? Certainly not all inhabitants of Tribal Reservations were cavalrymen in a past life, but there is always that possibility that some members of any tribe could be those previous soldiers simply for the experience of seeing life from a different point of view.

Past Life Trauma, Life Issues and Experiences

Now the next factor to consider is that of facing past life trauma, which will most likely arise as life issues in this current life, offering you an interesting opportunity for life-changing experiences. How will you handle these?

If a woman was raped in a past life, and was not raped in this life but came close to being sexually assaulted as a child, which did induce some level of trauma, how will she handle her relationship with men during this lifetime? This can surely be a challenging situation. But in this example, the woman does fall in love with a good and kind man who loves her deeply in return. They have children and both of them work diligently to protect their children from any sexual harm or abuse. In this (simplified) case, positive karma is created because the woman did not allow what happened to her to become a family pattern.

Take the man who was beaten by his father or mother over and over, yet he chooses not to beat his children, instead taking a much more enlightened approach to parenting.

Consider if your trauma was dying in a house fire that destroyed your home, *and your entire family*, in a past life. In this life, you are terrified of fire. Your challenge will be to learn to face this fear and to trust that you will be safe in your home. Perhaps because of this past trauma, you invent better smoke detectors or fire-fighting equipment. Perhaps you use the old trauma to make the world a better place.

What if your past trauma was physical? What if you were injured, were born with a terrible disease, drowned, died in a volcanic eruption or were killed by a tornado? What if you died in a war? What if your village was attacked by another tribe, or raiding party? What if you were living in France in 1789 during the French Revolution, and were beheaded for being on the wrong side of the political struggle?

Your past trauma could be that you suffered terribly as a slave in Greece, Rome, Africa, China or the Southern United States. Or you could have been sold into prostitution as a child, or just sold as a child for whatever reason. These are all huge traumas. If you find that this concept of slavery ignites a fire in you, use the power of that past experience to live a free life. Many people join the military to keep their country free of these types of issues even if that is no longer an issue. Others join the FBI, INTERPOL, or police forces to stop trafficking of children for the modern sexual slave market.

What if, life after life, you died in childbirth or saw your children die of starvation because of the traumatic conditions you were living in?

Experiences happen to us for one reason: the karmic lesson of the experience, even if we have no idea at the time what we should be learning. Traumas and events open a doorway for us to remember who we are and what we need to learn or improve in each lifetime. If you drowned in a past life, or many past lives, make it a point to learn how to swim in this lifetime and face your fear of water.

If your child died of starvation in a past life, learn how to be able to provide for your children in this life so that abundance surrounds you. You have been given a new opportunity.

If illness was part of your life, learn how to keep your body in excellent shape, including how to address the emotional issues that cause illness, as well as holdovers from past lives. It is possible that many miscarriages stem from the fact that women lost children in a past life and cannot face that potential loss again. Fear of the death of a child is a powerful carryover from past ages.

If prostitution were a part of your past life experience, and there are trigger points for you, then face that something happened to you and that way of life was not your original choice, and it no longer describes you in this life.

All the past life traumas, experiences and life issues offer each of us a Free Will opportunity to make a karmic change in our lives for the better.

Soul Purpose and Life Mission

Soul Purpose

What is your soul purpose for being here?

Why are you here? What is the meaning of your life?

Are a life mission and a soul purpose the same thing?

Soul purpose can be something as simple as living past childhood. Soul purpose does not have to be something seemingly extraordinary on the surface. It can be so simple yet karmically critical for that person's soul evolution. Here are some examples of soul purpose:

Perhaps in a previous life, a person died in childhood at the hands of child abuse. In the next life, living through a childhood in an abusive family and through the years of therapy to understand that childhood, could be the primary soul purpose for that person.

Dying as a baby or small child will offer all of your family members as well as other people this powerful experience of learning to work through grief, of learning on deeper levels the power and importance of love. The purpose of your death will be to offer you the understanding of the impact of your death on all those around you. It may appear to be a simple, albeit hard to fathom life purpose, but it is nonetheless extremely powerful in its karmic ripple effect. Everyone around your death will be given an opportunity for spiritual growth.

Working through health issues allows the soul an opportunity to more closely value their mortal bodies, to take a responsible look at what caused this to happen to him or her, and to work through this critically important issue. Perhaps in a past life the soul abused his or her body. Their soul purpose in this life will be to honor the new body with respect and care. This alone is a powerful karmic lesson. The next life may offer this soul a much stronger and healthier body.

A soul may have one or more difficult character traits that require adjusting. Some souls get a Ph.D. from the "school of hard knocks," as the saying goes, meaning that they make the same mistake repeatedly. The goal in one life would be to address a stubborn attitude, or the desire for abusive power over others, learn to stand up for one's self or to stop being so submissive.

Have you ever met a person who endlessly played mind games, or another who was constantly manipulating people for their own personal entertainment? It could be that that soul needed to see the harm he or she was causing and to learn to be more compassionate and humble. But the other purpose for this soul's existence would be to *offer others the opportunity to stand up to their mind games and manipulation.*

If a soul committed suicide life after life, it could be that in this current life, their soul purpose could be something as simple as not killing themselves. Living through the tough times, asking for help and learning to live a whole life could be that person's main purpose in this life. This is so simple and yet utterly profound for the evolution of that soul as the following example poignantly illustrates.

It's so hard you know? Through several regressions I realize that someone I loved died and every time that person left, I killed myself. I was never able to face life without him. One life he was my son, another my dad, or my husband or brother. I don't know why I have to learn to live without him. Why do I have to learn how to live with such grief? But, oh God it's so hard! My beloved one has died again in this lifetime too – in a plane crash. But now, I understand what I have to do. I can't just leave anymore when the grief hits me. I have to stay, to live, to grow. Tomorrow is my wedding day – to another man. I love him, but he's not like my beloved. This is a good man. I want to make him happy. Maybe my sole purpose of living this life is to live a whole life for the first time in a long time. Maybe if I learn this lesson, I can eventually have an entire lifetime with my beloved.

There are those occasions when a person's soul purpose is to live long enough to help another person get to a certain point, and then leave, die, exit the life stage so that the widow or widower can learn how to love someone new.

Other experiences make us appreciate life more. Not every soul experience is of profound significance or involves a death.

Can You Have More Than One Soul Purpose?

Do people have more than one soul purpose? Oh yes! Karma is never going to waste the energy of any mortal life. *Every single moment of life in a human body is pregnant with the potential for life lessons, positive soul evolution, spiritual growth or regression and raising or lowering our soul frequency.*

The example of the person who abused their body or who had repeated medical/mental health challenges may not be simply to learn to heal and respect their body. Their secondary purpose may be to serve as an example to others of the importance of maintaining that body, or the karmic effects of abusing a body. The ripple effect of that person's life purpose will endlessly impact those around them.

Sometimes a soul purpose is simply to be in the life of another person, to be present for that person as a parent, child, aunt, neighbor or teacher. The person may know this on some level but is usually not conscious of it. This person is everyone's Rock of Gibraltar. Their kindness, generosity, caring and helpfulness may be that steady rhythm in the background of the lives of those around them that enables others to *do what they do.* The secondary purpose may be an example to others of what stability looks and feels like *even if they are not conscious of it.* Others are able to see what sacrifice looks like and how others benefit.

Perhaps this is the point of the 1946 movie *It's a Wonderful Life,* with Jimmy Stewart and Donna Reed, that so many people watch every Christmas. The focus of this film was a despondent Jimmy Stewart who believed that his life didn't matter, that what he was doing was not important and that he had failed his friends and the customers of his bank in a time of financial collapse. But his friends and family rallied around him, reminded him of his seemingly mundane contributions to their lives and they showed him just how much *his life did matter to them all.* It's a feel-good movie because it reminds us to remember our goodness not our failings.

Think back through your life and look at all the life lessons you have experienced. How many did you have to repeat? How many can you say that you have learned? Could you say that you learned the lesson to such a level that the power of that lesson *lives within you?* How many people helped you on your journey in this process?

The Tibetans say that your enemy is your greatest teacher. Sometimes while someone's soul purpose may be to learn *not to be so cruel, karma is not going to waste the energy of this person's existence. This enemy to others may enable those others to learn how to stand up him or choose to be his victim.* Each difficult encounter is fraught with a myriad of potential consequences. The seemingly bad person may also learn to change their behavior based on the reactions of those around them.

Why do people join law enforcement or the military? Is it only to be a violent warrior? Could the reason be so much more mundane or more humble? Many join the military to have a feeling of belonging to something larger than themselves, to have the experience of being of service not just to their country, city or town, but to learn discipline, to learn to play the politics of an organization and to grow in it. All of these can be labeled as part of a soul's purpose for a particular incarnation.

Embracing each lesson raises your frequency a little bit here and there, and places you in a wonderful position to move forward and face more learning opportunities as your life moves ahead. Imagine not having to relearn those lessons in the next life, not having to experience that particular hardship in another life. It is so powerful to consider that we get to take all the lessons, all the wisdom that we have learned in each life with us when we exit our mortal bodies and move into the 4th dimension. If we cross over immediately, moving from the 4th to the 5th dimension of the Heaven World, we can then work with Counselors of Divine Wisdom to more fully understand the challenges and triumphs, gathered from the life just lived.

Life Mission

What is your life mission?

A **life mission** is different from a soul purpose. A life mission is usually undertaken by a more advanced soul, because he or she has possibly evolved beyond some experiences and has the karmic time and space to focus on a specific type of mission. This however, does not mean that the soul does not still have to work through other soul purpose challenges. It may be that some challenges that others face, this person no longer needs.

A life mission can be an area of interest that the soul perfects life after life and the range is tremendous, probably because on Earth, we need all kinds of skill sets to make the world work. Many souls return, life after life, to enhance a specific skill set. Consider these examples:

All civilizations are enhanced by the creative power of art. We are surrounded by art and some of the most memorable artists of all time may have been those souls with a mission to elevate the world by their art. Artists are driven to create: when this is denied, part of them begins to die. The opportunity to create beauty *is that person's soul mission*, perhaps life after life, leaving a legacy of beauty for all time.

Music is critical to raising the frequency of the entire world. Creating beautiful music that comprises the full harmonic scale in the wide range of music opportunities enhances all of us. Creating music is a tremendous soul mission as well as those who sing this music. The motion picture composers of today have offered the world many tremendous scores. The memory of music that echoes in our hearts can eternally lift us up. Imagine the karma of creating such astounding music. Some singers have a four-octave vocal range and have brought astounding performances to the entire world. Their powerful voices offer us not just an opportunity to appreciate their skill but also an opportunity to clear our minds and hearts.

Some politicians have arrived on the world stage at just the right time to bring their country to a greater level of stability, prosperity and social change. These men and women saw their life mission as a higher calling. We can identify them throughout time, be it Queen Elizabeth I or Golda Meir of Israel, George Washington, Abraham Lincoln, Mahatma Ghandi or Mother Theresa. These people forced the world to see the human conditions they were seeking to help.

There are military people who knew from a young age that this is their destiny, their soul mission and they quickly rose through the ranks to lead men and women, working to keep them safe all the while trying to carry out their mission of service to their country. General George Patton, General Douglas Macarthur, Lord Nelson and John Paul Jones are just a few of the men who understood why they were here.

Most medical people have such a strong desire to focus on healing in all its forms that they are often seen as driven people.

Some people may prepare all of their lives for their life mission and not fully embark on it until slightly later in life. Others reincarnate and embark on their life's mission as child prodigies in math, music, art, and literature. But not everyone is initially conscious of their life's mission. Some stumble upon it for some reason and awaken to why they are here. Everyone is different. However, once the person is aware of why he or she is here, usually that mission is pursued with intensity.

Remember this example of soul purpose: a person died in childhood at the hands of child abuse. In the next life, living through a childhood in an abusive family and through the years of therapy to understand that childhood, could be the primary soul purpose for that person. But what if that soul makes great strides and *takes on a soul mission,* that of being available to help other family members who would like to break that family pattern of abuse. This once abused soul will now have elevated him or herself onto a higher level of wisdom and insight. He or she *will have grown to a higher spiritual level of evolution and soul frequency.*

We all have many soul purposes and some people have those and a clearly defined life mission.

Life Mission: It's Never a Gift

Magnificent musicians, and creative composers are never "gifted."
Masterful mathematicians are not simply presented with a gift at birth that when they open it up makes them an instant genius.
Witty, wise writers do not receive a gift that tells them how to create great books.
Significant scientists, dynamic doctors and elegantly designing engineers are never gifted with fairy dust that makes them able to do the astounding things they do.
Insightful intuitives, the psychics among us do not receive the gift of the Merlin gene at birth that makes them see through walls and doors, have premonitions or talk to the dead.
The lauded leaders among us may study and learn but the ability to lead others lives within them. It was never a present they got to open, a gift card they received.

None of these abilities are gifts.
All of them are earned abilities that carry with them,
often significant karmic responsibilities.

Soul evolution means that as we evolve, we begin to focus on a certain area of ability or service that we can hone life after life. And because that person, that more advanced soul has that ability, he or she carries a much more significant karmic burden in *how he or she uses that ability.* Just because someone is brilliant does not mean he or she is wise. The soul is still evolving and may have honed one aspect of their ability and need to focus on continuing to evolve in another.

Global Changing Life Missions

Some souls have evolved to such a level that they can finally make a global difference by putting eons of life mission incarnations to tremendous use in one particular lifetime. Sometimes it all comes together and *the world needs that person at that particular* **moment in history.**

Where would the United States have been without George Washington, Thomas Jefferson, Benjamin Franklin, John Adams and all those players on the global stage that set up the United States? The United States: that flawed, struggling yet successful country that stands as a beacon of freedom to the world. Someone had to get this concept of democracy started so that hundreds of countries all over the world could begin to use the template these men offered to allow people to be free. They were the right men at the right time.

Abraham Lincoln was an extremely advanced soul. His wisdom and insight were critical at his point in history. Lincoln knew that slavery was a scourge upon the earth and had to be eradicated. He prosecuted the Civil War not only to free the slaves in the Southern United States, because he also understood that all the new states entering the Union would be forced to choose: slave or free. Lincoln wanted there to be no question: all men would be free in all states. Slavery had to be abolished which was why he pushed so hard to have the 13th amendment to the US Constitution passed: it formally abolished slavery. He also had a deeper vision of the future of this country: **at all costs the United States must remain intact.** He somehow understood that in the decades to come the massive power of the United States could become a force for good all over the world. If the Confederacy had won, World

Wars I and II would have had radically different outcomes. Abraham Lincoln's mission was to keep the United States intact. When that was secured, he left.

The Dalai Lama is a recognized person with an advanced soul mission: furthering world peace, not by advocating one religion over another but by advocating (not preaching) tolerance, and compassion, patience and love. He projects a powerful strength that the entire world relies on for subtle guidance. The High Lamas around him are also advanced souls whose mission is to further that of the Dalai Lama.

Mother Theresa was another advanced soul who took on a tremendously difficult mission: a Catholic nun in a Hindu country offering love and compassion to the dead and dying, to the untouchables. She was offering leadership, hope and death with profound dignity. This was no easy life mission.

Writers, composers, scientists and the anonymous people in all fields who are driven to create, change, advance, heal and help us all are the best examples throughout time of people whose soul mission was sophisticated enough to make a global difference.

As a soul evolves spiritually, he or she is offered greater and greater opportunities to perform *pure service to all of humanity, to further the spiritual growth or the physical safety of humanity.*

Can the reverse be true? Can a soul devolve to such a level that he or she is groomed to create horror in the world? Souls who are able to cross over receive the benefit of the guidance of the Heaven World. But souls who languish in the 4th dimension, making little progress life after life, are 'useful' to a darker intelligence. These "possessed by darkness" souls can be placed in a manipulated puppet-on-a-string political position to bring havoc to an entire country, continent or impact the planet.

These are not just dictators like Philip II of Spain (who

sent the Spanish Armada against Elizabeth I), Mao Tse Tung, Hitler, Pol Pot, the Korean family of dictators, or the ones in Haiti and various parts of Africa or the vicious priests, bishops and popes of the Inquisition throughout history. These are the purveyors of slavery, mass murder, torture and holy wars. These people have to come from somewhere and that somewhere is the Lower Astral environs of the 4th dimension. The master black magicians of the 4th dimension have spent eons perfecting their torture techniques and preparing their special reincarnating human marionettes to place on the world stage to create horror, death and fear.

It is as if the Light Side and the Dark Side face off. World War II was a classic example. Hitler and his global henchmen faced off with Churchill, Roosevelt, Eisenhower, Patton, Nimitz and the countless others who offered their best to save the world. These power brokers were all evolved souls in their own ways and it is important to understand how critical it is to evolve in a positive way: what a difference it can make to the world.

The Factors in Soul Evolution

Early Childhood Experiences

What happens to each of us as children colors our view of the world for our entire life and either enhances or impairs a person's soul evolution. It can be that one of that soul's purposes is to overcome or enhance these types of experiences.

The perception is that all babies are born "innocent" of any sin or darkness. Babies are just as subject to the laws of karma as adults are. Innocence is relative, meaning that a child will usually not remember their past lives and starts out each life, with what appears to be, a "fresh slate." Yet every soul enters mortal life carrying a "spiritual suitcase" of karma with them. Each new baby is going to arrive with many different "soul purposes" and possibly a life mission. Parents do not know what the karma of their child has been or will be. All any mom or dad can do is to be the best parent he or she can be to take a child to adulthood with the view of being a good person, a contributing citizen to the world and the ability to give and receive love. It is also a parent's job to ensure, to the best of their ability that their son or daughter is never abused in any way. But not all parents are responsible. Parents are working out their own karmic soul purposes and the introduction of a child offers endless theme and variation to everyone's karmic path.

Trauma from the time of conception can *potentially* cause a person to be fearful, timid, withdrawn and embrace a victim mentality. This trauma can be anything from the person being conceived in rape, not being wanted by either parent, having a drug-addicted mother, not receiving the proper in-utero nourishment, being abandoned at birth or being given up for adoption at birth or shortly thereafter. It would not be difficult to see how any of these life-initiating ordeals could color a person's view of the world. However, these events could be the karma the person has earned and has to embrace as their soul's purpose for overcoming and thriving. All of that is possible. The key element is free will. What actions will the person choose to take?

Some babies are so desperately wanted by their parents, that an entire family celebrates their birth. With super protective, hovering parents, this soul's purpose may be living with the smother love of controlling parents.

Babies born with cancer, birth defects, mental challenges or who die very early are all classic karmic balancing elements, which will be hard for the person and their families to understand. For example, when (not if) a drug dealer reincarnates, he or she may be born to a drug-addicted mother and be drug addicted himself. This woman may not have the emotional or financial tools to care for this child and the child could be placed in foster care. Consider the series of traumatic events that this seemingly "innocent" baby will experience so early in life. This karmic path can take this child down another dark hole or he or she can embrace their soul purpose, which could be to *overcome their rocky beginnings*. Needless to say, the karma all participants earn as each issue is managed will further or hinder everyone's karmic path and advance or regress their soul evolution.

Some children are so adored from the moment of conception that they have the karma to enjoy delightful childhoods, richly embroidered with fascinating and happy experiences. Trauma never touches them. It is wise to consider that they also earned this karma. However, their life purpose may mean that they are faced with other far more tremendous karmic challenges later in life and they needed the stability of that calm childhood to give them the foundation to face those later difficulties. These challenges may mean that this soul has more profound and spiritually/karmically advancing lessons to learn. This may be one of their soul purposes.

Child abuse may also be karmic. A child's presence offers an adult the karmic *free will* opportunity to abuse or not to abuse. If the adult chooses to abuse a child, then this will determine a great deal about both the child's and the adult's karmic path. At some point the child may stand up to the adult as the woman in this example did.

My father beat me every day. He beat my baby sister so badly that she developed permanent brain damage. I remember the day he did that. My sister was screaming and screaming. I was crying so hard, begging him not to hurt her and my mother was just standing there. She didn't try to stop him. Finally, my sister stopped crying. Only later did I realize that he permanently brain damaged her. Then my father beat me for crying. He beat me so hard that he always left large bruises. When I was in school, my teachers tried to intervene but my mother stopped them, saying it would be worse. My mother sometimes would leave him but she always returned. When I would sit sobbing and in pain on the floor she would stand over me and tell me I must have deserved it. I loved her. How could she do this to me? Finally, I grew to be six feet tall and he couldn't beat me anymore because I fought back. I survived him but I want to kill myself every day.

Was fighting back her karmic test? Was surviving childhood part of her soul purpose? This woman sought out psychological and spiritual help and she did not kill herself, surmounting a huge karmic challenge. She also learned that although her father beat her, the far worse abuser was her mother. This revelation, this insight may have been a huge step on her karmic path and possibly helped her to have a better life in the future. *She began to learn the lesson of those parents.* Eventually, she married a wonderful man, became a mother and was the kindest most loving mom. She effectively changed her karmic path *and her family pattern,* exhibiting the courage and determination to understand her family on multiple levels. She evolved to a new level. Her soul purpose may simply have been to survive those parents and learn from them. This simple statement is profound on so many levels.

Child sexual abuse is among the most severe forms of harm because this robs the child of their sense of security, the ability to trust adults, and creates a sense of permanent vulnerability in the person. But it is also a karmic test. How will the person face life after this? Some men and women seek spiritual guidance, work to create a deeper connection to God to find peace and solace. They do in fact begin to heal their lives. Some men and women make great progress while others seem to make marginal progress, but none of that is for us to judge. The karmic path of any soul's evolution is deeply private.

What happens if, as a teenager, you go joy riding and kill or seriously injure another person? The following vignette will illustrate how karma can work in these cases and how a soul can choose a powerful path.

I hate my father. He never wants to teach me to drive, but I learned, got my license and took my friends out for a little drive in my new jeep. I guess I'll never know why I did it, but for some reason I crossed the center line on a curve and had a head-on collision with a Mercedes SUV. Those folks were fine, but my best friend was horribly injured. For a while

I wanted to kill myself. I couldn't believe I did that. I searched, you know? I wanted to do something to make this sick feeling inside of me somehow go away, but nothing worked until one day I had an idea. I started volunteering at a rehab center for people injured in accidents. I learned how what I did affected people for years and years. I am so sorry, and I have learned how much compassion those injured people need. Now I know what I want to do, what I must do. I'm getting my degree in occupational therapy. I've made it my mission in life to help people who are injured. Maybe now I can atone for what I did. I don't feel so dead inside anymore. Maybe someday I can forgive myself. I hope that God can forgive me because I don't think my friend ever will.

An entire book could be written on the karmic aftershocks of the things that happen to all of us from birth to age twenty. Every single event echoes throughout our entire lives whether we had a great or crappy childhood. The key factor is how we approach the lessons we were offered from that early time. Our childhood offers us a myriad of soul purpose learning opportunities. One of the key elements to being on a spiritual path is the opportunity *to become aware* of the karma we create with our actions and reactions, lessons learned or not learned. This enables us to understand that our actions will continue to echo forward throughout our lives and into our future lives dramatically driving what our future soul purposes will be and eventually offering us the opportunity to take on a soul mission.

Current Life Experiences

Now that we know that the complexity of personality that defines us is carried forward from past lives, and new opportunities are presented to us from the moment of birth, it is time to turn our attention to our current life experiences.

I saw my father laying there on that bed, a wizened old man, full of cancer from the nasty cigarettes he smoked and the tobacco he chewed. He was so frail, so helpless. I hated him. He beat me with his belt buckle from the time I was a two. He had no heart, no soul. He berated me, made me feel as if I was worthless; he destroyed or tried to destroy every good thing I tried to create. It was as if for his whole life I was his whipping boy. It would be so easy to kill him now. A syringe full of air would kill him in seconds. He's going to die anyway. I wanted power over this son of a bitch. I wanted to watch the fear in his eyes as finally, I had power over him. I wanted to watch his eyes as his heart exploded, I wanted him to know that I had finally returned to him, the hurt he had tried to drown me in. I contemplated my next action. He couldn't speak because the tongue cancer made that impossible. He could barely breathe because the cigarettes had destroyed his lungs. I saw fear in his eyes. And then it hit me: he has no power over me anymore. If I kill him, I will be no better than he is, I will have become him, and all that he said about me will be true. I could still feel the pain of those whippings. I could still feel my humiliation as a child when I would wet my pants when he came toward me: but not anymore. Now, in spite of him, I am successful. I am married to someone who loves me, who is compassionate to me. I have brought up my children away from my father. I became the father I wanted him to be: loving, caring, a teacher for my son and daughter. Maybe I had evolved past him. Maybe I am finally free of him. I watched him lying there, alone, and afraid of death. I left him there, alone, and walked out of the room. He will die by his own karma, not because I killed him. I am free now, truly free.

Sometimes a person's life is defined by that one moment when the soul's purpose for living awakens within him like a bright dawn. This is what happened in this case. This man may have thought that his life had been defined by his father's cruelty, but what defined his life were the free will choices he made, who he chose to become, and what kind of father he decided to be to his children. He undid the shackles of emotional prison his father had kept him in by realizing he had redefined himself long ago. Imagine how far he evolved. His soul purpose would seem to be surviving and surpassing his childhood. This is huge progress.

Think about your experiences. Did you merely consider yourself lucky or unlucky?

Think about your decisions over the long or short years of your life. Marry those decisions to your perceptions of being lucky or unlucky. Do you see a correlation?

I have always considered myself such a "sweet" person. I believe myself to be kind and loving. But it's so weird – all my life I have felt as if people took advantage of me. I don't know, maybe that stemmed from my father's abuse when I was small. I didn't want to be like him. He victimized my mom. She never stood up to him. I like to make peace, give people what they want and make everyone happy. When people do things to me, I just walk away; I don't like confrontation. I don't want to get upset. I just don't get it, though, why do people keep taking advantage of me?

Learning to stand up for what is right, for your own rights, is among the most profound lessons any of us can learn and it is a significant soul purpose. This woman became just like her mother, frozen in place, unable to stand up for anything. It is so critical that many people come back, life after life, simply to learn this one lesson, this most basic soul purpose. Because if you cannot stand up for yourself, those around you never feel safe and you serve as the example of someone who not only sacrifices themselves but also those around them. Karma will eternally place this learning opportunity in front of you until you finally "get it" and take action.

Mortal life offers us so many profound lessons, and what we embrace and fully learn may not have to be repeated in future lives. Some of these are the most basic examples of a soul purpose:

- Standing up for yourself

- Learning gratitude
- Healing grief
- Opening your heart to compassion
- Healing your body
- Loving your body
- Standing up to abuse
- Using your skills and abilities wisely
- Not playing mind games to have power over others
- Recognizing your strengths and weaknesses
- Imagining how other people are going to react to your actions
- Being a teacher
- Sharing
- Learning to forgive
- Changing abusive behavior
- Turning away from bad decisions
- Rising to the occasion when you are in a crisis
- Not being afraid to love
- Not being afraid to love again, after a divorce or death
- Refraining from judgment when we seldom know the entire story
- Thinking before taking action
- Seeking wisdom
- Recognizing when something is not yours to do
- Seeking to atone for past mistakes
- Learning to be kind
- Evaluating choices before making decisions
- Facing your fears
- Facing your failings
- Facing your emotional frailties

- Acknowledging your strengths
- Continuing to embrace the intellectual pathway of learning.

This is a tremendous, yet incomplete, list of potential soul purpose opportunities that all of us will encounter at some point in our centuries of lives. Each person, place and even will offer us a chance to learn more about who we are, who we can become and the karma we are creating for this and future lives.

There is a fascinating nineties movie with a funky title called *Groundhog Day*. In this film, the lead character lives the same set of circumstances over a 24-hour period over and over, and over and over, until he embraces the soul-purpose lessons he is there to experience. He learns to stop being so sarcastic, to be kind, to brilliantly play the piano, to understand love, to be compassionate and to see himself for the jerk he had become. Ugh, that sounded judgmental, but others perceived him as a jerk and no one wanted to be around him. *Only when he embraced each life lesson fully, only when he had satisfied his soul purpose,* could he move forward with the next day of his life. In those moments, he raised his frequency, embraced the karmic opportunity of the moment and changed his karmic path forever.

The premise of this movie is the classic example of what we each go through: when will we learn to be better than we currently are? How many eons of lives will it take to stop any of our chronically detrimental behaviors?

But there are also amazing lessons that people are allowed to enhance. Someone had a soul mission to figure out how to replace internal body organs rather than letting someone die from a diseased liver, pancreas or kidney. Now, organ transplants are among those things that we can routinely take for granted, but someone had to pioneer this concept, perhaps someone who had a life mission life after life to save people with organ failure. But karma never wastes energy and the life mission to save people also impacts those who may be saved. The technology of this time period has enabled many doctors to embrace and provide mitigated healing for thousands of patients. Mitigated healing means that the patient had the karma to receive the organ and the soul purpose opportunity to embrace the reason they needed an organ transplant in the first place. Now karma is offering this person a level of healing which means that he or she *must honor the new organ and must do things differently in their life, otherwise that organ may fail as well.* The organ could fail for many reasons, but if the person does not change key things in his or her life, this could play a huge karmic part in that success or failure.

Some people are consumed with a desire for service. This feeling becomes this person's soul mission. An interesting example of this is the desire to help people to help themselves by creating a structure for affordable housing that is safe, beautiful and feels like a home. Socially minded people all over the world have taken up this critically important mantel of service.

Consider the life mission of a Dutch inventor by the name of Boyan Slat. While diving in Greece, he found himself among more plastic than fish. He determined at that point to create a system that will clean up the oceans of the world and help to preserve the planet's priceless ecosystems. His systems are currently at work cleaning up the oceans. This is a life mission of service to humanity in a different way. This man's journey along his path of soul evolution is greatly enhanced by this powerful and world-changing idea.

Mortal life is filled with theme and variation of experiential opportunities for the furtherance of a life mission or the challenge of a soul's purpose. Karma and free will are the key elements here in how this will all play out.

40

Karma Created in This Life

Every moment we are alive builds on the next moment. This statement is not made to create paranoia within us but to make us awaken to, be conscious of and be responsible for our actions. Often when we think we have an opportunity to be happy, something comes along that snatches that happiness from us and places us at a crossroads: what will be our next step? What choices will we make?

I remember watching Princess Diana's life as it played out in the press in the 1980s and 1990s. It was the fairy tale: the handsome prince, the gorgeous young girl, and the fabulous power of the House of Windsor. What a life awaited her! But billions of us watched as her life unraveled. She was an emotional mess. The world may have loved her, but her in-laws and her husband did not. She was not educated and had no idea what her job was other than to be the Princess of Wales, but it seemed to me that, despite all of this, she tried. Even after she was divorced, she took on a much larger job, helping people in Africa by bringing attention to the land mine issue, furthering AIDS research and teaching her sons how to reach out to people. I have often pondered what her karma was in this life. Did she die too early or was her job done?

No one here can judge the life of such a famous person. That said, however, it is fascinating to watch the progression of a person who originally had no ambition in life, no focused education to do a specific task, much less a life mission, who felt unloved all of her life and was among the loneliest people on earth at her death. And yet, despite all of that, she did appear to embrace a life mission: using the power of her position to display compassion for people suffering. Her causes were not neat and tidy. She held the hands of AIDS patients during a time when no one even wanted to touch them. She brought attention to and showed on television people who had lost limbs due to land mines. This yanked away the politically correct facade of charity by a royal person. She was in the spiritual trenches trying to do good work for others.

And she was not alone. Her sister-in-law, Anne the Princess Royal is considered today among the most tireless royals when it comes to performing service for others. In fact, Princess Anne, supports the patronages of 332 charities that span the globe. Her tireless efforts have quietly, without fanfare, changed the world, clearly identifying her life mission. Both women used and continue to use the power of position to help others, thereby creating tremendous karma for themselves because of their dedication to service.

The great master, Dr. George King, of the Aetherius Society, declared that we are here for service to others. Service in any way to other people, even in small ways, creates positive karma and raises frequency/vibration. This legacy will empower that soul to perform greater and greater elements of service in future lives, dramatically enhancing that person's soul evolution and shining an extremely bright light on that person's karmic path.

Soul-purpose experiences are also part of every single soul's karmic path. No one on earth can escape these opportunities. Perhaps you are performing tremendous service, but your marriage no longer works and you get a divorce. You will have to grieve the end of this relationship and learn how to embrace a new relationship. You may have to learn compassion for your spouse, help your children understand the circumstances and help your friends and family avoid gossip and judgment about your situation.

A person's life mission may not be entirely positive or spiritual. Some people make it their goal to become the richest, the strongest, the most famous, or wish to become the most powerful people in the world. These life goals earn unique forms of karma. Let's say that you decided to embrace some of these less service-oriented life missions and along the way, you ended up crushing those who "got in your way." You became a rich, powerful and charismatic politician who abused women, or compromised the security of your country or who made a chronic series of thoughtless decisions, or consciously caused the murders of thousands or millions of people. The elevated position of this person puts them in a place to create a karmic ripple effect for millions of people directly and indirectly *throughout time.* The karmic ripple effect that will be returned to this person will echo out – not may but will definitely echo out – in unimagined ways for thousands of lives in the future. Why? Because the law of action and reaction has to be obeyed, whether a person is conscious of this law or not. Ignorance of any spiritual law does not eliminate the karma the person creates by violating that law. Free will decisions by any human being in a position of power *will create unimagined karma in the future, especially if these decisions create harm to others and/or the planet.*

Once a person embarks on a spiritual/karmic path of awareness and he or she begins to learn more and more spiritual truths, *this person is held to an even higher karmic standard of action and reaction.* Once this person is unequivocally conscious of these laws, then the karma created when these laws are violated comes at a more intense level: the person cannot say he or she does not know.

The priest told me that my parents were living in sin because they practiced birth control. I was nine years old. I didn't know what "birth control" was. He told me my parents were going to hell. Only he could help me. I believed he was lying to me and I told my parents. Why would a priest tell me that? Was he trying to separate me from my mom and dad? When I look back on that situation, now that I am so much older, I realize that he may have been preparing to abuse me. If he could separate me from my parents, then he could easily separate me from God because that is what I have seen priests do to the people they have sexually abused. I was lucky. My family left the church. What was his karma?

Priests, clergymen and teachers, who *know the power they have over children,* create intensified karma. This is especially true for the clergy, because separating a child from a parent, and then God, deprives that person of any spiritual solace in addition to the sexual abuse. The karma created by this is significant. How that karma will be returned to that clergyman in a current or future life is not something any mortal can calculate. However, in the example above, that child helped that priest's karma by reporting him and by not allowing him to abuse her any further. This experience will have definitely shaped that soul's spiritual path, causing her to look at those in a position to have spiritual influence over others, far differently than she would have ever done before. Karma certainly did not waste energy with this memorable experience.

I've been on the force five years now and police work is hard every day. You see the worst of humanity so many times and often you see people when they are going through the worst day of their lives and yet you have to be kind, compassionate and detached. I try to help. Sometimes I wonder about people. Am I making a difference? I wanted to protect and serve, you know like it says on the side of my patrol car, but sometimes I feel abused by the public and yet they call on us when there is a crisis, domestic abuse and accidents. I had no idea this job was so hard. I wonder sometimes if it's worth it.

Service actions create karma, whether the person realizes it or not. Yes, you met someone on the worst day of his or her life and you did help. You did help that person out of a burning car. You did stop that drunk driver, even if he threw up on your shoes. In every moment you gave your best, you maintained your ethics and you upheld your job. You also will have garnered deeper insights about yourself, and if you have any depth of self-awareness, you will have faced many soul-purpose lessons. Embrace them. Work through them. Did that domestic abuse case remind you of your parents? Was that child abuse case reminiscent of how your neighbors treated their kids? Now you can help. Now you can make a difference in the lives of those people. Yes, even when you leave, people will still be perpetrating terrible things against one another, but for the people you have helped, their lives are better and the positive karma you created for yourself will be of tremendous value in the next life.

Karma never wastes the energy of any moment. Every action, gesture, comment or non-action creates some level of ripple effect. The more conscious you are of those effects, the more you will be able to positively affect your karma.

How much karma can you create for the future if you die early?

He was just 26 years old and I still can't believe how this happened, you know? He had just come back from Iraq, served two tours and he got out of the Army. Said he'd had enough of the killing and the horror over there. I told him I was so glad he was home. He said he wanted to do things that helped people here and he was staying with me, looking for a job. One Saturday he was in the park, walking my dog when he saw this man smacking a little boy around. Kid was about – I think he said, about eight. My Leroy, he walked up to the man and he asked him to stop, said it wasn't right to do that to just a little kid. The man left, real angry. The child said that man was his momma's boyfriend and he hated him. My son befriended that child and they would meet every afternoon to toss a ball around. The little boy started to laugh and smile a whole bunch more. Then one day, that boyfriend of that child's momma came back and started beating the boy again. Leroy asked the man to stop. Next thing that happened was that thug, pulled out a revolver and shot my son straight through the heart in front of that child. Then he calmly walked away, cool, like no one would tell him what to do – that's what the witnesses said to the police. I'm heartbroken. If my son had died in Iraq, he would have been a hero, but he died here, murdered, and no one thinks he's a hero.

But he was a hero to that child.
He did die in the service of his country and heroes do
not always wear a uniform.

One of his main soul purposes may have been to die
in the service of another, whether it was here or in Iraq. The
karma he created standing up for that child, even though he
died in the process, earned him tremendous positive karma. He
changed that child's life and since there were so many witnesses
to that premeditated murder, that murderer went away to serve
life in prison. The energy of this man's sacrifice didn't need a
medal, a uniform, or even recognition, because karma *always
recognizes the service and sacrifice one person gives to another.* This man
will be afforded the opportunity to be of greater service in
another life. We also do not know what karma was satisfied by
his death, or how this death will echo out, changing many
different futures. People living in this dimension, in ordinary
day-to-day lives, will never fully understand the depth and
dimension of how karma echoes out into the future.

Take a quiet moment and ponder the buffet of
experiences you have had in this current life. Now ponder each
decision you made and how you exercised your free will in each
of those times.

Free Will

Free will is the concept that every decision you make
is based on your freedom of choice in choosing any option.
This applies to everything in your life from driving a car, caring
for a pet, entering into love and relationships, parenting,
working, creating, inventing or just walking down the street.
Your brain is constantly *deciding* which side of the street to walk
down, which store to enter, whom to speak to, whom you will

grace with your smile, which purchase to make, how much money to spend, who will receive the purchase, where will you put it, and on, and on, and on. Every second you live as an adult is a decision powered by your free will.

When does a person learn about karma? From the moment of birth you are guided into this free will decision process by the life path you have as a baby. Over time, awareness takes over and by the time a child is 18 months old, parents must begin to mold the decisions a child makes so that wise choices are the preferred option. But not all parents can responsibly guide a child. Some parents are terrified that their child will not love them if they say "no" to a toddler's or child's choices. The soul purpose for this parent may be that this mom or dad has to learn to love his or her child *enough to learn to say no to them because setting boundaries and limits keeps this child safe and enables them to become a responsible adult.* This all starts at this age.

The karmic consequences of allowing a toddler of 18 months or similar age to be allowed to do whatever they want because the parent is fearful of tears or saying no are tremendous. It's the difference between rearing a great person and creating a monster.

Karma, or the law of cause and effect, the law of consequences, begins to be part of a child's life when the parent starts to teach them what happens when they say or do something that is unsafe, or is not part of societal norms, or when they lie, destroy toys or other things, display willful behavior and/or hurt another person. Creative parents find ways of teaching the consequences of actions. This is the child's initial foray into the world of karma. Normally it comes naturally in the course of simply raising a child. But most people would never consider that they are teaching a child how to exercise free will responsibly. The parents who never teach a child this crucial lesson ends up wondering where they went wrong, why their child or children will not behave or why these same adult children hate their parents.

I was so thrilled to have a daughter that, well, I know I spoiled her a little bit. She was just so cute I couldn't say no to her. Is that so bad? Now she's having trouble in school. She's unruly, breaks things, screams at people and bites other children. I'm afraid if I tell her no she won't love me anymore. I never believed in reprimanding a child. I always believed that the freedom of spirit would allow a child to grow up naturally and be a child of God, a child of nature. But I guess that isn't so, is it? Now I have a monster on my hands, and to be honest, I can hardly stand to be with her, she's so impossible. She hits me, spits on me and screams at me. Did I do something wrong?

Free will applies to parents: teach your child to behave or watch as that ripple effect comes back to bite you – literally. Evaluate the choices you are making and have made as a parent. Ask for guidance, then exercise your option to discipline your child by teaching him or her the consequences of her actions. Guide her in wise choices. Both of you are creating karma but parent karma, in this case, is more intense than the child's karma *because the parent is expected to know better.*

Free will can be exercised, even in a military setting, especially if the perception is that *the exercise of this action will be for a greater good, even if it gets the person into trouble at the time.* Sometimes you simply have to seize the karmic moment.

He's going too fast. We shouldn't be going all ahead one-third in the harbor, in the fog, on the surface! The Captain's showing bravado to the Inspection Team, trying to prove how good our submarine is, but this is madness. This is dangerous. Oh my God! Now he's ordering me to go all ahead at flank speed! I know this means the end of my career but I have to refuse. I cannot in good conscience do this to my fellow officers and crew members. Here goes:

"Captain, this is dangerous. I will not take the ship up to that speed. I'm making a log entry that on this date, I, the navigator of this ship refused a direct order to take the ship to flank speed because it is

unsafe and this constitutes an unlawful order."

The Captain becomes enraged and screams at me.

"Navigator, this is insubordination: you're relieved! Executive Officer take the ship to flank!"

And he did and when we collided with another ship, the sail of our submarine sliced that civilian freighter open like a can opener. The Inspection Team relieved the Captain and the Executive Officer on the spot, for cause. They were both court martialed. I was reassigned and my career was intact. I can't believe it. I did the right thing and even the Navy acknowledged it!

But what if you exercise your free will and you believe you have done the right thing and you still feel as if you are being punished?

I'm so excited to be pregnant! I'm a nurse in a big hospital, so I know all the things to do to take care of myself. I love my job, so I plan on continuing to work as long as I can. I heard a rumor recently that they are requiring all nurses to take the flu shot, but I'm sure they don't mean pregnant women. Those shots are full of mercury and my doctor warned me against the danger of mercury for my baby. I'll talk to my supervisor. . . I'm stunned: she said no exceptions. She blithely said that my baby will be fine even though there is not only mercury in that vaccine, but also all kinds of other things that are not good for a developing fetus. She threatened me: I either get the shot or I'll be fired. I refused the shot and she fired me on the spot. I know I've done the right thing for my baby and myself. Why do medical people tell you no mercury and yet insist you get injected with it when you're pregnant? How can this be right? I feel like I have done the right thing and now I am being punished. Punished by them, but I feel that I chose the life and health of my child over my job. I'm okay with this decision.

Free will decisions mean that you have to take responsibility for your choices, even when they have what at first may appear to be dire consequences, like job loss. But had she allowed mercury to harm her fetus, she would have carried the primary karmic weight of that decision instead of the hospital. All those in the chain of command at the hospital would have also carried karmic weight, but the mother will always carry the greatest level of that responsibility for the aftermath of the shot. If the child had developed a mental problem or a chronic illness, the mother would be responsible for a lifetime of care, not the hospital. The mother looked into her (karmic) future and made a critical choice.

Free will means that often consequences of actions are immediate and unexpected.

She stabbed my 10-year old daughter with a pen knife in class! I want to sue the school, and the teacher, and the parents. This is assault! How could this happen? What's wrong with that girl that she goes around stabbing people? I'm so angry I can't function! I want to punish that family but somehow that doesn't feel right. I have to think about this. What will I do? (Calming down) What is the best action for the greatest good? Why would a 10-yea- old girl stab anyone? If I sue, she won't get any psychiatric help, just blame. What do I really want for my daughter and this other child? Am I responsible for this child too in some way by how I handle this? The lawyer said we have a year to sue, and we can, but we can also make specific demands of the other child's parents. So, this is what we want: the child must apologize to my daughter in front of the entire class, then this assault incident must be entered into her permanent school record and finally, she and her family must undergo an entire year of psychiatric treatment to find out why she would do this. (A week later) The family agreed. I hope they find out why this child is so violent and I hope she can be helped. My daughter will have a permanent scar from the stitches and quite a story but she will be fine. I feel as if we have made the right decision. This was the greatest good for all of us.

Anger clouds free will judgment and it is critical to get past anger to think clearly about the decisions a person must make especially when a family member has been assaulted. But those decision choices will reverberate out for a very long time. In the case above, perhaps the little girl needed the psychiatric attention and her behavior was a desperate cry for help, and this was the greater good. Lawsuits don't always solve the problem and can make a bad situation worse.

Sometimes it is wise to consider that all of the free will decisions we have made throughout the ages are echoing throughout our lives today in ways we could not have imagined. Each time we reincarnate, we are experiencing the aftermath of each of those decisions with all the people we positively or negatively affected. Karma gives us untold opportunities to exercise free will to move forward with grace and wisdom, or with occasional hits and misses, or with one bad decision after the other.

Soul Frequency

Everything in all of life, in all of the seven super universes is based on math. Everything can be equated to some type of mathematical formula and that includes our souls. The mathematical measure of our soul is our frequency or vibration. Dr. Ibrahim Karim, in his study of nature's own design language which he calls Biogeometry®, discusses the *mono-chord*. The law of resonance is the concept of harmonics or frequency. When you think of a stringed musical instrument you can see that each note sounded along the line of that string is going to provide a different note or tone. Now imagine a string of infinite length: this is the mono-chord.

The higher we progress on our spiritual path, the more we are dedicated to ethics, service and building that divine connection to God, the more our level of tonal resonance with these character traits rises.

We are all striking all kinds of chords on a daily basis, based on where we each are on that cosmic mono-chord. Not all of us are in resonance with each other. We find that we seek out those who are like us, who share our "vibe" or vibration/resonance. That old expression "birds of a feather flock together," means that we are comfortable with people who are like us.

What becomes especially interesting is that as a person progresses on his or her spiritual path, the soul may find that they no longer share the same resonance with the people, places and things that they previously found comforting. This soul's frequency has changed and in the course of time, this person finds new friends, enjoys places of higher vibration and embraces more in-depth study of metaphysical elements that affect their life. *They changed. Those around them did not and they were no longer in resonance.*

One of the fascinating elements of vibration is that the higher a person's vibration, the more healthy, happy and balanced this person feels. They are better able to handle problems, see and sense the best path and seek wisdom before embarking on any action plan. Now as their frequency rises, very often their intuitive ability also rises, offering them a greater sense of connection with the higher elements of their spiritual path.

The reverse is also true. If someone is beginning a downward spiral, they may find that they are no longer in resonance with their friends and that people who had previously stood by them are simply no longer there. People turn away, not because they are callous or unfeeling, but because when you are not in resonance or sharing the same vibration, you can no longer can communicate on the same level as you once did.

The study of vibration, resonance, frequency and the cosmic mono-chord offer us an opportunity to see ourselves in a larger picture and to consciously decide that we can change our lives, raise our frequency and move forward on our spiritual path of soul evolution.

The Complex Soul

Are we new souls or old souls? We are all old souls and our karmic path is based on our level of soul evolution, soul frequency, the karma we have created from our past lives, our past life traumas and experiences, and the powerful need to face certain life concerns. A critical overlay is the list of soul-purpose challenges we must each face, and for some of us, we have to push forward with a critical life mission. As we begin each new life, we are molded by our early childhood experiences, and as we mature, by our current life experiences and by every karmic moment we have lived in this life. All of our decisions are based on our free will to choose how each moment will be spent. None of us leads a perfect life. We are all caught up in the web of our past lives and the reincarnation cycle.

Our Soul Evolution is an ever changing, evolving or regressing process. Now as we evaluate these concepts, perhaps it is important to enter a deeper world of understanding of our past lives and how reincarnation affects our soul's evolution.

What Is a Past Life? What Is Reincarnation?

Why Do We Reincarnate?

We reincarnate because it simply is not possible to have any soul fully appreciate the process of soul evolution without the opportunity to return to mortal life again and again. All right, let's say that you committed a terrible crime in the last life. What could happen in the next life? You could be confronted with another opportunity *to make a different choice in the next life.* This is the beauty, and the generosity of reincarnation.

What if you were a doctor in many past lives and you experienced tremendous frustration because you could not save a soul entrusted to your care? Imagine that in each life, greater discoveries would afford you the opportunity to save this person the next time. Consider how much a person has to learn simply to get through medical school. Perhaps these men and women can grasp the sheer volume of information to assimilate *because they remember much of it from past lives.* This is why it may be that doctors reincarnate life after life and practice some form of medicine, simply to be able to save their patient the next time in that next life. The irony here is that it would surely behoove them to study karma as well. No physician, healer or shaman can ever save everyone. Death balances karma as readily as life.

Reincarnation is the concept of life energy or soul energy moving to a different realm after death. Then, after a specific time in that realm, reviewing the life just lived and hopefully understanding what was learned in that life, a new birth vision is created. After that, the soul is returned to the physical plane in a new incarnation or "reincarnation." The soul is reborn again (and again and again) to gain new experiences and to fulfill its "birth plan" on its karmic path to soul evolution.

The main argument that *establishes* rebirth is one based on a profound understanding of the continuity of mind.

Where does consciousness come from? It cannot arise out of nowhere. A moment of consciousness cannot be produced without the moment of consciousness that immediately preceded it.

All consciousness is energy.

All thought is energy.

This is the concept that energy is neither created nor destroyed.

Our consciousness can never be destroyed. It always exists as a clear light inside us. It is who we are, *and we know it.*

"Good Lord, he's so familiar! I know I know him, but how? I can feel my heart pounding in my ears! This shouldn't be happening, but it's real, it's such a powerful attraction. I'm engaged to someone else and now all of a sudden I know I won't be marrying that man. This is the guy. Something about him is so comfortable, as if I've spent a lifetime with him, and yet we've never met before. How can this be?"

56

"I love Italy. I love the food, the climate, the art, the language. I've never taken an Italian lesson in my life and I feel as if I just know what's being said. Oh, and even in Naples, that manic city by the bay, I'm never lost, never feel overwhelmed; I'm at peace here. What is this feeling?"

"I remember that the first time I met her this rage erupted in me, this feeling of anger, of violence, came roaring to the surface of my consciousness. I wanted to run as far away and as fast as I could from this monster of a woman, this nightmare personality who would become my mother-in-law."

"How does my daughter know how to play piano like that? We've never given her a single lesson and today we visited a piano store and she sat down at a piano and began playing Mozart. What six year old does that? What's happening here?"

What's happening here is the power of past lives to influence our current daily lives. It happens to us constantly, whether we are conscious of it or not. We may never have brought that awareness to the surface and given it a name. But it has a name: reincarnation.

The Bible and Reincarnation: Life Everlasting

Many Christians piously point out that the concept of reincarnation does not appear in the Bible – saying that reincarnation is an Eastern philosophy only.

History tells us that the Emperor Justinian and Empress Theodora decreed in the sixth century that the concept of reincarnation was to be considered heresy and they had it removed from the New Testament Bible. Imagine the karma of these two individuals who, with one swipe of a pen, removed one of the basic foundational elements of all religion: faith in Life Everlasting, the future and belief in past lives. Prior to this time, priests, bishops and other high-ranking members of the

Christian movement fully advocated the concept of reincarnation, the crucial belief that we are all held accountable for victories and defeats from past lives. *The hope that our previous good deeds will be rewarded and acknowledged, and that the karmic system of justice will balance the scales of cruel deeds and horrific crimes, is the fundamental basis for reincarnation.*

Perhaps this would explain why every other major religion/faith on the planet teaches some aspect of rebirth. The belief in the power of karma, or justice, is essential. Perhaps even more important is the concept that there is no physical way that one soul could possibly gain all the experiences necessary for enlightenment and soul evolution in one lifetime – especially if that life is brief. The need to grow, to understand and to mature as a soul is paramount. The comfort in knowing that if we are unable to get it right in this life we are given another chance is an essential element in the concept of a compassionate and loving God.

The Group Karma of Family Drama Factories

Each person who re-enters mortal life comes with several soul purposes for how that soul will live his or her life. Some less-evolved souls may not have a very specific birth plan for the length of their life. However, other souls are very deliberate and focused on what they have decided needs to be done in this life to further their soul evolution. We decide each time we reincarnate that we will have specific purposes to fulfill, specific patterns that we wish to break or specific dramas we wish to escape. We are all souls in a growth process, and sometimes the power of another person's purpose can impact us greatly. We have had previous lives with all of these souls, the eternal experience of group karma.

And we remember them. We remember those people and

those events by some method that causes them to be imbedded in our soul, our very being. *We know, because we have done it before or lived with that person before. Our soul remembers things for eternity.*

We remember these things because our subconscious is an eternal recorder of all of our soul experiences in both life and death. Our subconscious mind never sleeps, never takes a day off, and is recording even when we are under anesthesia. It is this memory – this eternal photographic, auditory, full sensory array of memory methods – that travels with us as we are born, die and are reborn. We are in each life, the sum total of all of our previous life/lives experiences. Fears, abilities, strengths and weaknesses give form and dimension to our personalities. We are who we have always been, and yet we are ever changing, evolving personalities, *based on who we used to be, now with hidden memory to offer us an opportunity to do things differently, better, with more courage, skill and grace, in each new life.*

When we die, our soul leaves our body, transitions from the mortal realm to the 4th dimensional realm. Some people make the transition into the Heaven World, but most souls do not, instead languishing in the 4th dimension until they eventually reincarnate. We do not take physical things with us, but we absolutely take with us the irrevocable memory of every single moment we have experienced and in every single life we have lived.

Memories are never destroyed.

Memories help guide our path, help us to make decisions and allow us to learn from past experiences, even if we do not consciously have that memory at our fingertips.

Families are drama factories! We may be born with our soul purpose safely tucked away in our subconscious, but once we are plopped into the midst of the drama of the family that welcomes us (hopefully), sometimes our most well-intentioned plans can become almost immediately skewed. The power and complexity of life is what happens to all of us as we are making other plans.

Many souls reincarnate as children of extremely abusive parents. These souls are just sure that *this time*, they will be able to overcome this terrible family pattern of physical, verbal, emotional or sexual abuse. *This time*, they will leave that family behind and will burst forth to become a person who is totally healed. Then this soul's plan calls for him or her to then turn around and help other souls trapped in toxic family drama to make their escape.

It is a most optimistic and honorable plan, which requires tremendous courage just to survive the terror-producing cruelties of childhood. These souls are sure that *this time* they can survive that vicious father or murderous mother. *This time* they can avoid that lecherous priest or grandfather. *This time will be different.* The soul is filled with righteous resolve.

But when the soul is faced with a towering series of cruel, crushing, tragic events, little bits and pieces of the soul begin to go numb, begin to shrink back and go into survival mode. Sometimes layers of a soul are sheared off, fractured. The soul is diminished. If a soul survives a situation but is so traumatized that he or she cannot make any meaningful changes in their lives, then the soul will begin a physical, mental, emotional and spiritual decline. There is only so much help that this soul can receive or can hope to absorb in a single lifetime. Sometimes people this damaged have to die, *cross over into the Heaven World,* and then reincarnate. However, if this soul does not cross into the Heaven World, then those sheared off bits and pieces of that person's soul will not be restored in the time out of the body. That person will return often a more broken person than he or she was in that previous life.

This soul's evolution will have made marginal progress. All the players will get to return to make this work again because karma generously provides continued opportunities to work through these dynamic family issues.

Facing the Family Dynamic

How can you be sure that this is true? Think of a family that you know where there is chronic dysfunction. Is there at least one family member who has broken free of the dysfunction –fought the pattern and emerged more whole and balanced? Family patterns continue life after life. You see this in specific patterns such as rape – rape victims are raped life, after life, after life. Abortion appears as a family pattern, as does poverty, cruelty, abuse - verbal, physical and emotional. Wealth is also a family pattern, but the acquisition of wealth may not be done with integrity, and that family pattern may need to be broken as well. This means that the tremendous wealth that the family heirs receive may need to be used to atone for the harm done in acquiring that original level of wealth if many people were harmed in that process.

Many times we have heard of people saying that they want things to be different for their children than it was for them. They want more for their children than they had for themselves. They want to be able to provide more progress on many levels. Unfortunately, people usually think of this in terms of material goods, but frequently there is the desire for more spiritual growth. They may not call it that, saying that they want more balance, more happiness, more of a feeling of belonging and being at peace with themselves. Thankfully, there are people who are successful and achieve a better balance for themselves and their children than they had. Examples include people who do not abuse their children as they were abused, stop the incest in the family, break poverty consciousness or approach great wealth with a social conscience of generosity and caring.

Let's take an example of a family of great wealth where on the outside peering in, all seems perfect. Big house, gorgeous family, plenty of charity events: the perfect life. But if you look closer, you see that the dad is maniacal in his desire to control every family member. A seething rage is just below the surface inside each sibling and his wife. The husband routinely does often gross, humiliating things to his wife at big events. He controls all aspects of his children's lives, even his married children. He seems to be a classic narcissist. His wife is determined to change him, to make him into the perfect husband. She tries everything and finally she realizes that she has to stand up to his abuse instead of eternally making excuses for him.

This is hard for her. In several past life regressions, this husband has murdered her when she tried to stand up to him. Abuse can span many lifetimes. But with help and encouragement, she realizes that she is teaching her sons that it is okay for husbands to abuse and she is teaching her daughters that it is normal to accept the abuse. So, she moves out of her 10,000-square-foot mansion, gets her own place and continues her volunteer work. Her husband is astounded. He didn't believe she would do it.

He promises to change if she returns. She holds out and demands to know how he will change. He can't believe she is serious. He tries to fill her with guilt for "abandoning the family," but she is not deterred. Only when he finally agrees to meaningful changes does she return. It took several years of transition, but he *did make the change. The family has changed centuries of patterns by both parents making fundamental behavioral alterations.* It would appear that both souls have now evolved to a new level, satisfying their soul purpose: change their behaviors toward each other. It is wise to note that this process took over twenty years to work through. However, in cosmic time, that is light speed.

Everything in the spiritual world seems to be a process, or the act of processing energy. Reincarnation is no different, but how does it work?

Well, first you are born, or first you die _ which comes first matters not. For this discussion, we will start with death or going home. This is important, because the concept of death as an end is not quite correct. The physical body dies: the soul lives forever.

How Do We Know There Are Past Lives?

When Tina was a child, her mother was watching the Art Linkletter show. He had, as a special guest, a family from India. This is their most intriguing story:

It seemed that almost from the day she was born, their youngest daughter was trying to return to a different home. She learned to speak early and eagerly spoke of a life in another part of India. As the story emerged, she described in detail her husband, her children, her home and her strong desire to return to this family. They needed her; she left them too soon. No amount of consoling helped or lessened her desire to go back to them.

Finally, when she was five years old, she begged so insistently, that her entire current family journeyed to this other part of India to find this "past life" family. She accurately described the part of the country they entered before they got there. She gave exact directions to her "past" home and her excitement grew as they came up to the house. Her father knocked at the door of the home of his daughter's "past" family. A man answered the door. The little girl ran to him, called him by name and told him how much she had missed him and asked about all of her children – whom she also accurately called by name. The homeowner was astonished for he had never seen this child before. The little girl's father explained to the man the circumstances of how they came to be at his front door. They were all invited inside.

The past life husband asked the little girl if she knew how his wife died - yes, she replied correctly, by pneumonia.

He asked her details about each of the children – she got all the answers correct. Finally, the past life husband said that the true test of her identity as his previous wife, would be if she could locate the jewels his wife hid just prior to her untimely death. The little girl went directly to the back yard and dug them up. The past life husband finally was convinced that this child was the reincarnation of his wife - who had been dead for about six years.

Laura tells the story of when she and her then 6 year old daughter were window shopping and they came across an Eastern Imports store.

All of a sudden, my daughter stopped and stared inside. She asked if we could go in. I told her, of course. She became unusually quiet. She looked at a display of Tibetan Prayer flags and in an almost trance-like state said, "I used to hang these up when I lived in Tibet." The shopkeeper and I just looked at one another. My daughter then went on to tell me all about the myriad of icons, Kwan Yen, Buddha, the different types of Buddha statues and what they meant. She talked about how hard her life was in Tibet, but that she loved every moment of it. She talked about how she would carry buckets of water to her home every day. She also told me that I was her mom in that lifetime, too. Then she started to cry. She became overwhelmed with a sense of homesickness for a life in a land that I had no recall. In fact, I don't think she had ever even heard the word "Tibet" in her current 6-year lifetime. I knew my daughter was recalling a powerful past life.

"Why Don't We Remember Our Previous Lives?"

Blessedly, we do not remember our past lives because we can start out somewhat fresh with each birth. We do carry with us the resonant frequency and karma from a previous life, but it is better that we do not remember the details of the previous life that is currently impacting the life about to be lived. Unfortunately, we also forget that we are part of the Divine.

Aha! Enter religion! We are also born into some type of faith so that we can explore all kinds of experiences with that faith. Could be that this is why there are hundreds of belief systems on this bright blue planet? There are many paths back to the Divine, back to God.

What often happens is that people get mid-way through their lives and realize that they could have done things differently so they begin to think about this. Often, they have made *seriously* poor choices and wish that they could have a do-over.

Think about how many times people say that "If I had it to do over, surely I would handle this situation differently, or love more, or be kinder or take a different path . . ." What each of them is really saying is: *if only I had a second chance.* Well, we all get a second chance and a fifth and a twentieth chance. This is called *reincarnation.*

When we are born, a *veil* comes down that causes us to forget our past lives. We are then given the opportunity to do it over, with a fresh slate, meaning that we are presented with almost all the same circumstances that led us to make a poor choice in that last life. Then we are given a choice: will we do the same thing all over again? Will we repeat the pattern or will we change the future by doing something completely different? Changing the pattern, doing something differently, better, wiser is the surest path to soul evolution.

This is the point of the karmic path: the opportunity to try again and again. Human beings come in as imperfect souls seeking wisdom through the process of experience. Understanding this will hopefully give us the necessary insight to *be different, think differently, act creatively and break that often, centuries-old pattern.*

If the etheric body of the mother is of a very low resonant frequency through the use of alcohol, drugs, tobacco, or any type of abuse, this can directly affect the etheric structure of the developing fetus. Trauma can also affect the new baby including accidents or physical traumas caused by the mother or the father.

Perhaps it is unnecessary to remember our past lives. We are responsible for every action we take in each life. This means we manifest what we need to learn.

When we stop needing the lessons of poverty, we will be wealthy in all aspects of our lives, not merely financial.

When we stop needing illness, we will be well. There are a thousand lessons to be learned from any illness.

When the student is ready, the teacher will be there. When we need to remember a past life to help with a lesson, the memory will be available to us.

Sometimes that past life memory *is* the teacher to help us understand a lesson. A friend once had a chronically difficult relationship with her sister. They could never get along and there seemed to be no logical reason for their intense dislike for each other. But one sister kept studying the problem and finally realized that she and her sister had had a past life with each other. It felt like this flash of recall was a sudden insight that awakened her to a different possibility for understanding her sister. She had an awareness that the chronic hostility her sister exhibited *felt familiar,* as if it had happened in other lifetimes. She never received all the details of that past life together but she gained enough insight to be able to approach her sister differently. She was able to grow from that experience and ended up having a more than civil relationship with her sister, much to the relief of the entire family. They couldn't undo what had happened in past lifetimes, but they could use the present to fashion a brighter future. While they may not be best of friends, the tension and high emotions are now faded memories.

Many great ones have stated emphatically that is it not necessary to remember your past lives to move forward in this life – focus on the present, not the past. For the vast majority of people, that is the truth, but for some people, the key to the future may lie in understanding the past.

An amazing cellist performed around the world, delighting audiences with her professional style and emotional performances. However, before every performance her anxiety would go through the roof. The situation was becoming increasingly paralyzing. However, after a past life regression, she learned that she was a Jewish child during the Holocaust who had to perform for the Nazis. If she did not do well, she faced execution. What drove her to play in this lifetime especially if it caused her so much anxiety? Perhaps the skill she earned in that past life needed to be shared with the world and it became spiritually necessary. It became her soul purpose for her to overcome her anxiety to move on with her life. Fortunately, she did get resolution from that past life memory recall and her performance anxiety left her.

Gift or Memory?

We are all connected to everything around us. Each connection attaches some type of memory to our very being. We carry with us, in our etheric structure (also called our auric field), the memories of all we have ever seen, everyone we have ever known and all the places and things we have ever touched or visited. All of our experiences are the very essence of our memories. These memories are connected and stored in our solar plexus. This is why a very ancient memory from a past life that comes up suddenly can create an instant nausea in us. Some memories are so powerful, so negative, that they can make us sick. Consider this challenging situation:

A neighbor of mine has a child who was about to study abroad in Spain. The night before he was to leave, he became violently ill. His mom called me to see if I could help so he could be able to get on the plane that next morning. As I "looked" at him, I saw a portion of his history unfold before me. He was the same age now as he was in this past life. However, in this past life, the Inquisition was persecuting him. They cut his eyes out. His subconscious was freaking out about returning to this place of horrors. However, karma puts us all in interesting positions from time to time. I wondered why karma would send him back there. Were there lessons he was to learn for his spiritual growth? I didn't know and it was not mine to know. I was merely put in a place to help him with his illness and worked with his subconscious to calm him down. Then I sent him with a team of angels to protect him. He went on the trip of a lifetime, and never had an issue while he was in Spain. I never told either the child or the parents of his past life. My job was to help him with an illness and that was all I could karmically do.

This is important to understand because we carry within us, in our etheric body, all the memories of all the lives, all the experiences we have ever had. This means that when we absolutely need to, we can access those memories to help us grow or overcome a past hurt, trauma, fear or guilt.

Those memories are stored in our subconscious memory archive. Since your subconscious never sleeps, never forgets, never stops accounting for every moment of your existence, in every life you have ever lived, your soul recorder never turns off. Even during surgery, where you are anesthetized, your subconscious is still recording the event. It remembers every single moment, every person, place or thing: *forever.*

People call these memories our Akashic Records, the sophisticated name for the archive, and some people think that only psychics have access to our historic memories. But it is unnecessary to go to a psychic to access those life records. They already belong to us. Often a past life regression may open up a past life volume from these Akashic Records, so that you can gain insight into what is happening to you in the current life.

It also means that if we *just know* how to do something, it is not a *gift*, it is a *learned ability*, honed over many lifetimes. And this *ability* carries with it specific *responsibilities* for its use. You frequently hear people speak of someone having a particular "gift" of psychic ability, music talent, medical insight or artistic talent, or anything for that matter. These people worked on these skills over possibly hundreds of lifetimes. They *earned* the knowledge or skill they can now access, so seemingly effortlessly, and they built upon this knowledge and/or skill, life after life. It is wise to remember, that *gifts* are returnable. The abilities that *live within you* are *earned* and are *not returnable and you cannot turn them off.*

What If a Regression Doesn't Work?

Sometimes a past life regression attempt doesn't work. There are many reasons for this; however, the most logical one is that the person may not be at the right karmic time or opportunity to have a certain memory recalled. The reason for this is not a fault. It is something that we must merely accept on faith.

Karma allows us access to our Akashic Records for specific purposes at specific times. The "veil of forgetfulness" comes upon us at birth so that when we get our "do over" in this new lifetime, we will be allowed to freely make our choices without the specific memories from past lives. People need to believe that there is an opportunity to do things again, but in a better way. Well you are living your do-over. You don't remember so that you can use wiser judgment in this life. Sometimes not remembering your past life is its own blessing. Choose wisely.

It would also be wise to forgo allowing any psychic access to these Akashic Records. No psychic can ever know *for sure* if what he or she thinks they are seeing is correct. Also, you should attempt to stop someone who just decides to blurt out what your past life was or who you were. How do you verify that information? Whatever he or she says to you is going to influence you and that influence incurs karma – usually not positive karma. In addition, someone telling you what he or she thinks was your past life may be using this "special knowledge" to have an unsavory influence over you. Own your life, your memories and your Akashic records. Take charge of your soul evolution. You can read more about this in the section "Beware the Egocentric Psychic."

How Do I know If I Learned the Lessons from Previous Lives?

If you look around and you have: great health, a happy outlook on life, abundance (which can take many forms), children (if you wanted them), a wonderful love life and fulfilling work, then obviously, you have overcome many patterns. If you have all this and you are still seeking other types of experiences through service, giving love and compassion, then it is possibly safe to say that you have come a very long way and are, perhaps on your way to realizing a life mission. You are in a great position to soar in your quest for greater and greater insights, understandings and opportunities to do more service.

What if the opposite is true? What if you are having a terrible time finding someone to love? What if wealth constantly escapes you? Want children but cannot have them? Have one terrible boss after the other? Have kids and a husband, but find that you are not happy with your life? Perhaps it is time to consider that there may be some elements of your past that you may want to bring to the forefront of your consciousness and begin to address, understand and work to heal. Finding these answers could be numerous aspects of your soul purpose.

The more knowledge you seek to acquire about your life, who you are, why you are here, the nature of your reason for living, your purpose for being here, what you want to accomplish, and what experiences you want to have, the more of all of these will you have. Who are you on the inside? Do you like who you are? No one can make any of these assessments but you, and all of them are influenced by the karma you came in with and the experiences you had in one or many past lives.

This concept is even more powerful if you know it, if you are *aware of it* and consciously seek to expand your knowledge from life to life. It is unnecessary to consciously remember a past life to expand on it. All you may require is the desire to continue to expand your knowledge in one particular area.

"Can You Cure Present Day Illnesses, Phobias and Fears by Exploring Past Lives?"

Yes, sometimes you can, but it depends on the nature of the illness. A past life regression is an opportunity to "regress" to a past life through either hypnosis or another form of meditation process. No regression process is exact. You are "regressed" to the life that you may need to see the most, not a life in which you would seem to get all the answers to your questions. Often a regression will open up more questions than answers. And sometimes a regression will show you something completely unrelated to what you think you were looking for.

One of the tests of whether or not you have an issue that can be addressed by a past life regression is the degree of effort you have made to resolve the issue and the success you have had before you ever consider a exploring your past. Not all past life regression efforts will resolve a physical or mental health issue. Nothing works 100% of the time.

You never know what a regression will show you. Sometimes a past life regression will show you seemingly nothing significant, but in some unusual cases you can see that it is unnecessary to "go back" at all. You are doing just fine – you may find that you are doing so much better than you could have imagined and your subconscious and your higher self will prevent you from returning to any past life. This is a message to look at the present and the future for your path.

However, there are many documented cases of past life regressions working remarkably well to heal a present life issue.

One woman had endless stabbing back pain and finally, in a regression, was shown a past life as a gladiator in the Roman Coliseum. Her death at that time came from a massive sword attack in her back. Once she was able to see this, and the heavy dagger was symbolically removed, her back pain vanished.

A person being persistently overweight may stem from a past life whereby he or she perished by starvation and dehydration.

One client observed how fearful her son was of water. He was eventually able to enjoy bath time, but swimming pools inspired terrible fear. A child of five is too young to do a past-life regression. However, it is possible that he could have died by drowning, perhaps in a pool or other body of water, in a past life. In adult past-life regressions, many people who have a fear of water discover that they did die by drowning in a past life.

There was also the unusual case of the man who had a grating, raspy voice. He almost sounded as if he were being strangled or was being prevented from speaking. He found out that he had been beheaded in a past life and his current difficulty speaking was the present-day aftermath.

One woman consciously remembered being thrown out of a third-floor window by a priest during the Inquisition. Her chronic fear of heights, as well as her hatred of the Catholic Church, could have been the current day result of this past-life experience.

Any unexplainable fear, phobia, chronic insomnia or sleep disorder, could stem from something horrific that happened in a past life, especially if it happened at night: perhaps a village was attacked or the person was killed by a criminal. We die in such a variety of ways that often an extremely traumatic death can create a lingering problem in a future life.

What Is an Unprovoked Fear of Another Person, Place, or Thing?

When two souls meet each other for the first time in this life, and they have an instant dislike for no apparent reason, this may be a past-life connection. Perhaps this person is a parent, a mother-in-law, a sibling or future spouse. He or she could be a boss, a neighbor or a new acquaintance. Whatever their current role, the subconscious recognizes that soul from another place and time and an element of that memory, part of our Akashic Record, comes to the surface. You may not necessarily remember where you know this person from, but it was not good. Remember, the reason that you are placed together again is to work things out with this individual or perhaps to steer clear of them if they are dangerous. Maybe he or she requested another chance to be a better person. Perhaps they want things to be different this time. It could be that they may have not changed much and you go through the same trauma all over again. You have the free will to change your own karmic path in this scenario. Instead of doing the same thing as you would probably have done in the past, take a different road.

You frequently see this in spouses who murder each other. Most people are killed by someone they know, or whom they have known for many lifetimes. There is the fascinating story of a woman who discovered that she had been raped in a past life and, to her utter astonishment, discovered that the rapist in that past life was her father in this life. She found herself stunned by this revelation because in this life he was such a great dad. This is a classic example of karma allowing both parties an opportunity to heal the past by offering them a chance to balance the karma and the experiences between them.

Is There Any Way to Prove a Person Lived Before?

One of the most startling discoveries to come along in a very long time, centers on an archeological dig in Gough's Cave in Cheddar Gorge, Somerset, England, in 1903. Here the discovery of the 9,000-year-old body of "Cheddar Man" was made; this was the most complete ancient skeleton ever found in Britain. Bryan Sykes, a geneticist at Oxford was trying to see if he could extract any DNA from Cheddar Man and compare the genes of modern Britons to the pre-agricultural hunter-gatherers of Cheddar Man's time. Modern technology in 1997 afforded Sykes the ability to extract DNA from Cheddar Man's tooth. Then he asked local residents to participate in the DNA comparison. However, there was only one match, a man named Adrian Targett. Adrian is a history teacher at Kings of Wessex Community School in Cheddar, England.

After analyzing a 400-nucleotide sequence of mitochondrial DNA in the samples from Cheddar Man, to his utter astonishment, Sykes found that Adrian Targett and Cheddar Man *differed at only one spot on the entire DNA strand.* The two must have shared a maternal ancestor, perhaps someone as close as Cheddar Man's mother. *Targett lives just half a mile from the cave where Cheddar Man was discovered.* While Cheddar Man was discovered in 1903, the concept of analyzing his DNA took place almost 100 years later in 1997. One of the interesting ironies for Adrian Targett was that he had applied for 50 teaching jobs all over the country, but the only place that he happened to get the job was in Cheddar, England.

What happened here? Is Mr. Targett the reincarnation, *9000 years later* of Cheddar Man? How amazing to have such a perfect DNA match, and for Mr. Targett to live only one-half mile from what may have been his "original home" and his ancient burial site. Does this prove he lived before? You decide.

Consider the children born in the 1950s who remember dying in the Holocaust. Those records are often traceable, and many people who lived from the sixteenth century forward in time can also be traced. This may not particularly matter to anyone except the super non-believer, who just has to have even more proof. Frequently those people will not believe you no matter how much proof you have. What matters is that if you remember a significant past life, that you get something out of the memory. Perhaps this need to remember results in an understanding, a release of fear or emotion or guilt, something that helps you to heal in some way in this lifetime and furthers your soul's evolution.

What Is the Reincarnation Cycle?

The reincarnation cycle is believed to be around 152 years or so. It can be much longer or significantly shorter. Some people have returned in as little as five years. However, the Tibetans believe that a person can come back almost immediately depending on the life review, karma and the need the soul has for specific life experiences. One of the most interesting theories regarding this is the anomaly of the "Baby Boom" after the Second World War.

Many people did not pay particular attention to the rather large influx of new babies until the sixties. Then an amazing phenomena manifested itself. These baby boomers were dead set against the Viet Nam war, and war in general. They made a huge drive for peace; these were the flower children of the sixties. But who were these souls?

The theory is that the over 70 million people who died in World War II did not have a chance to truly live that life and so the turnaround time to reincarnate was sometimes as little as one to five years. This explains why the children of the fifties and sixties hated war – they had just died and had to start all over again. It was almost as if you could hear them thinking: *never again will there be war.* But the Viet Nam war took another partial generation of young American men. These reincarnated WWII souls ran for office to stop wars, tried to open the world up to the New Age movement and make peace the paramount policy. They (we) were not always successful: the effort is still ongoing.

We have all met people or know of people who do remember their past lives. Some examples of them include a German tank driver with an overwhelming interest in WW II; Denise Linn, a past life regression therapist who believes that she died at Auschwitz; submarine personnel who continually have nightmares of drowning; pilots who remember their planes going down; Navy personnel who have recurring dreams of Pearl Harbor; Prisoners of Wars in the Pacific who died at the hands of the Japanese; children who died in prison camps – and the list goes on.

The most amazing aspect of this is that you can go back and trace these people. If you remember a specific death, some records can be verified. One man kept remembering being in a submarine. He remembered the name of the submarine and the names of his buddies who died with him. This information was eventually traced, and he was correct on every point. Ironically there is even a picture of him and his eyes are *exactly the same*. In this case, he even looked up his original parents from the forties. He did not contact them for fear that they would be too upset by his reappearance.

However, one man, who remembered dying in WWII, *did* contact his original birth parents from the 1930s. This was so bizarre, because he had parents from the 1950s yet he sought out his birth parents from that previous life. They lived in a small town in the South. When he introduced himself to them, there was an instant recognition and then a flood of tears of gratitude on both sides. Their collective subconscious remembered each other. These families came face to face with the reality of reincarnation.

Other people experience a longer reincarnation cycle. Take the man who kept having problems with ghosts from the Civil War. Apparently, he was a Civil War doctor for the Union Army and ran a small hospital in Virginia during that war. He reincarnated in the 1950s and again began to study medicine although his medical process took a more homeopathic route. He was looking for new ways to heal those poor souls he could not save in that past life. Although he was not told that he was a Civil War physician, a friend found a photo of a group of Union Army Civil War doctors and there was his picture, plain as day. Everyone who saw it recognized him. You can read this entire story in *Ghost Stories from the Ghosts' Point of View, Trilogy, Vol. 2.*

One woman remembered her heritage in a past life in Africa. She wore a white face with dark hair in this life, but she clearly remembered being an African warrior in a past life. She talked longingly of that life, of being in nature and life with wild animals and her tribe. She noted that she never felt comfortable in her "white body" in this life.

One man grew up in the humid southern part of the United States. He kept commenting that that climate never felt comfortable for him. When he moved to California, the land of high desert, low rain and no humidity, he immediately felt more comfortable as if this climate was closer to his heritage in a past life than where he had been born in this life.

The Process of Reincarnation:
Death Is a Beginning

Panoramic Life Review

Almost immediately as the soul is exiting the body, he or she watches as all the experiences of their entire life pass before their eyes in one blinding flash of emotion and sound. It's as if there is a video in a person's head that is triggered by the soul leaving the body. The soul receives a farewell look at the life just lived.

Some people feel an instantaneous "rush" as they are pulled back to their moment of birth, riding their first bicycle, greeting a sibling, the first day of school, their first sexual experience or their first abusive moment. Some are shown their marriage, and their children, the major events that defined their lives in one astonishing flash of light and emotional sound.

Emotional sound, that astonishing description, is what you feel as you watch your entire life pass in front of your consciousness in one rush of tremendous speed. You *hear* and *feel* your own emotions and then you are empowered by some means to hear and feel how others viewed you, and how you helped them or hurt them. Some people at once feel judged and yet no one is specifically sitting in judgment of you. You find that you are ultimately judging yourself. The entire process takes no more than a moment or two, and yet the sum total of who you were, what you did, how you were perceived, what you learned and what you could have learned, is spread out before you in one astonishing instant. This can be beneficial or quite uncomfortable. Most souls are completely unaware that this is coming and are not prepared to understand it – to welcome it and not to fear it. It is a view of how the soul progressed in the life just lived.

What Happens When You Die?

The process is the same for all mortal people. Slowly but surely the vital heat begins to leave the body if you are dying in a peaceful setting. The body begins to shut down, rather like someone who is the last person in a building: all the lights are shut down, all the mechanical processes are turned off. The body systems, specifically the nervous system and the circulatory system, start shutting down. If you are extremely fortunate, you fall into a coma and you exit the body. Then you stare back at the body that housed you, that carried you through this incarnation and you are either proud of how you cared for this mortal structure or you feel sad at the condition in which you have left your body. You create karma by how you treat your mortal frame, how you respect it or disrespect it. That karma has to be balanced in the future.

But death hasn't quite come; the silver cord is still attached. The silver cord is that amazing wisp of etheric cord that has magically attached your soul to your mortal frame.

Now as you look around you, you can still see the mortal people who were with you. You begin to think of the people who are not present and as you think of them, *instantly*, you are standing with them. And, in an amazing number of instances, they can feel your presence.

You find yourself ricocheting among all of your friends and family members. An astounding sense of freedom sweeps over you as you realize that you are completely unencumbered by that physical body. You are flying with the speed of thought. This situation can last several hours. But finally, the last vital heat has left the body and the silver cord becomes cut.

Once this is severed, you are declared dead. It is at this point that the soul leaves the body. This process happens over many hours and days or it can happen instantaneously if the person is in a crash, has a heart attack or is in an explosion or other intense trauma. If there is trauma the person will still travel with the speed of thought among friends and family members.

At some point, though, that traveling ceases and the soul is no longer just standing by a loved one. Eventually most souls move deeper into the 4th dimension, or as it is called in the 23rd Psalm, the Valley of the Shadow of Death.

Entering the 4th Dimension

The 4th dimension is a place of no time, space or gravity. It is generally extremely dark, although a majority of souls do see a light, but are not sure what to do or how exactly to get to that light. This is perhaps why the 23rd Psalm came to be, to guide us to the light. However, if the soul feels that he or she did not live the kind of life that would have earned them the path to the light, in an unfortunately large percentage of cases, the soul simply languishes in that 4th dimensional darkness. They are unaware that crossing into the light of the 5th dimension would offer tremendous healing, hope and counseling.

Souls in the 4th dimension become ghosts. Some know they have died; others will never figure it out. Some souls know they are ghosts and some ghostly souls have denied the concept of death for themselves. They simply cannot believe they have died. They wander the area where they met their demise and unknowingly haunt the living. Some souls who are aware of their deaths still haunt the living, moving in and out of the darkness but never making any spiritual progress. They are still incurring karma because of the harm, fear and interference they cause the living to experience.

Some souls are held in the 4th dimension, by the powerful attachment of the living, who are unable to allow their loved one to transit into the Heaven World. Some murdered souls are held to the Earth plane by their murderers. Only the power of someone specifically seeking them out to cross them over can begin to free them from the bindings of their torturer/murderer. Using *The Crossing Over Prayer for a Murdered Loved One* can be of tremendous service. Again, this specific prayer is available on **GhostHelpers.com**.

If the soul lingers in the 4th dimension, he or she may find that they are quite alone, or other souls may be seen if this is a group karmic death, meaning that many people died together, all at once like a plane, train or car crash. They are also cold, unsure of what to do next and cannot find anyone to help, guide or heal them: a sooty darkness embraces them.

Souls can reincarnate from both the 4th and 5th (Heaven World) dimensions. Souls who return to mortal bodies from the 4th dimension, carry with them the unhealed emotional scars from their most previous life. Many times, they return in as little as five years. Little progress in soul evolution can be made when reincarnating from the 4ᵗʰ dimension.

Souls who do cross over from the 4ᵗʰ dimension, enter the 5ᵗʰ dimension to find a world of peace, healing, guidance and hope. They are also allowed to re-invigorate themselves for up to a thousand mortal Earth-timed years before returning to a physical body.

How Heaven Restores Your Soul

It is a tough concept to embrace, but ghosts incur karma by their actions and non-actions. This is why assisting them to cross over is of critical importance.

Souls who move toward the light find an indescribable feeling of love, warmth, welcome and hope. There is a golden, dynamic quality to this light, almost as if the light itself were alive with love. All people find that someone familiar is there to meet them ***if they immediately cross over into the Heaven World***.

Once the soul is in the Heaven World, he or she may experience a more in-depth life review, where advanced spiritual beings help this soul appreciate the life just lived and give guidance on how to restore his or her damaged emotional parts.

All of this points to one fact: in death we cannot escape who or what we really are, who we have been and the kind of life we have lived. This is an element of the inevitability of karma: *eventually we come face to face with ourselves and how we are evolving as souls.*

Perfect souls only exist on the higher realms and even these Enlightened Beings are in a process of evolution. Those of us who are merely mortal, never lead a perfect life. We lead lives of experiential events. Therefore, the Heaven World's "panoramic life review" gives each soul an opportunity to "review" what was learned from the free will choices made in that specific lifetime and to understand what needs to be done differently, perfected or learned in the next lifetime. Most souls experience a profound sense of peace. Every single lifetime offers astounding opportunities for spiritual growth, wisdom and hope. This is true even if we lived but a few brief moments, dying at birth or being aborted before we even had a chance at life. The abortion situation would offer the experience of seeing the emotional turmoil our mother would have experienced, and perhaps compassion for her would have grown within us, even as she denied us access to that lifetime. Even a brief life and the life review, open the door to a huge range of spiritual lessons.

Hopefully we will learn compassion for ourselves and others. We may learn patience, and gain insight, so that better choices can be made in the next life. If you had a life very well lived, then, perhaps in a future life, you will seek to perform even greater service for mankind.

How Does the Process Work?

How many souls are there available to reincarnate? There are believed to be roughly 60 billion souls available for reincarnation on this planet at various times. But no one can know the exact number.

How is it determined where and with whom we will reincarnate? There are a tremendous number of determining factors for any soul's reincarnation. These include:
- Whether or not someone crossed over into the Heaven World after death.
- If the soul languished in the 4th dimension between lives, life after life, very little spiritual progress will probably have been made and the soul may return in as little as five Earth

years.

• Karma created in multiple past lives has a direct bearing on reincarnation time, place and group karmic ties.

• The interim between lives.

• How many experiences were gained in each lifetime?

• What critical lessons were learned in each lifetime?

• The needs of other souls to be part of a group incarnation.

• Sometimes the soul will need to experience a premature birth, or an early death as a child, in order to gain all the specific experiences to have a much longer life at another time.

• Which part of the world will be required for certain experiences?

• Does this soul have a role to play on the world stage?

• Is this soul needed on the world stage at a particular time?

• Does the soul need to be of a particular race and/or religion?

• Are the soul's skills required at a particular time in history?

• Will it be necessary for this soul to sacrifice her own development to facilitate the development of another? (A classic example is the soul who dies at birth or as a child to give an entire family the experience of this death.)

We do have it to do over. We are reborn to face our murderers, our abusive parents or our torturers. We are offered new opportunities for service, compassion and teaching others. Each pairing of souls is an opportunity *to make different choices in the next life.* This is the entire point of karma and reincarnation.

Rebirth

Whether it is from the 4th or 5th dimension, once it has been determined that the soul has to return to mortal status, the soul may decide on their soul purpose. Then parents are selected for the soul based on a resonant harmonic level, and the incoming personality watches the parents come together. What this means is that if you are not in some level of harmonic resonance with your birth and/or adoptive parents, you cannot be born into that family. Then near the end of the pregnancy or even up to two weeks after birth, the soul may enter the body.

Returning to mortal life can be within a short time in earth years, or centuries. One of the biggest determining factors is the dimension from which you are going to return. Souls returning from the Heaven World traditionally have a longer rest period.

As mentioned before, souls returning from the lower astral (4th dimension) can come back very quickly without any healing or soul restoration. This is a powerful reason to make sure that you and your loved ones cross over.

How is the rebirth time determined? The scheduling of rebirth is a rather complicated aspect because it involves group karma. Many lives have to be lined up correctly so that this soul can make his or her entrance. Most souls are eager to return to begin their next set of experiences and to work off karma.

Once the soul and his or her birth family are all correctly lined up, then an amazing mystical action takes place wherein the soul communicates with an element of Creation to coordinate the introduction of the spark of life that represents conception.

Many mothers had dreams in which their future children visited them. Often, the child will tell the mother their desired name as well. Frequently the soul of the child watches from the other realms as their parents work to conceive them. Not all conceptions result in birth. There are far more miscarriages and abortions than births, two factors that greatly influence the soul's karmic path. Many times, women miscarry for numerous reasons and the soul is denied access to this family of life streams. Other times, women deliberately stop a soul's access to this life through abortion.

You cannot kill a soul. Souls are eternal: miscarriage and abortion simply deny a returning soul's access to that family for the experiences he or she would have had. There is also the possibility that the soul can return to this mother at a later date and become her child. The timing and responses to these situations determine whether any soul will have access to working out karma on the Earth plain in a particular historical period.

The incoming soul can see how overjoyed their parents are at their impending arrival, or the extreme hardship this birth can create for them. This is true for adoptive mothers as well. We pick our parents, including our adoptive parents. We have to reach our chosen parents somehow and often adoption is the method. Karma offers theme and variation in how we will enjoy our life. Biology does not always make a family and many children given up for adoption were *supposed to end up with their adoptive parents for that experience.* Yes, the birth mother had free will: keep the child, offer the child up for adoption, or terminate the pregnancy. Each choice carries karma, but not always the karma we may think. In these situations, we cannot know the karma created or satisfied by each choice.

Abortion and Miscarriage

Not all women are meant to be mothers.

Not all women have the karma to be mothers in every lifetime. This is not good or bad, right or wrong. It is purely a facet of karmic timing.

Karma determines if someone will not ever be a mother or be a parent merely for a specific moment in time. Reincarnating is all about timing.

If you experience a miscarriage, then the soul who was to come to you at that time will have to wait for another time. No one considers that the experience of a miscarriage murdered or killed a soul. Something happened in the mother's body and the soul was denied access to that mother. Usually the mother has no idea what triggered the miscarriage action. In many cases, that mother may eventually go on to have children. The Clear Light of the fetus' consciousness is usually not impaired in any way.

How does abortion play into this alignment if the 'Clear Light' inside us, which is consciousness, cannot be destroyed?

Conception is an opportunity for a soul to reincarnate in a physical body. Abortion stops that opportunity, but it cannot destroy the energy of that soul who expected to join that mother's body. Souls are not destroyed by abortion any more than they are by miscarriage. Souls are eternal. The difference between abortion and miscarriage is that, with abortion, the mother made a conscious decision not be a mother at that time and terminated the pregnancy *for whatever the reason.*

Karma is created in both situations: however the karmic burden is significantly greater in abortion, because the mother's, and often the father's, free will specifically denied the life of the incoming soul. There are two ways to view this denial

92

of life by whichever means. In the miscarriage situation, perhaps the incoming soul did not quite have the karma to be born into that family with that mother at that time, or the mother did not have the karma to have that particular child. That does not mean that this soul cannot join that family at another time. The karma of abortion can also mirror miscarriage: perhaps this child did not have the karma to come to that mother at that time.

At other times, when a mortal soul decides to have an abortion, this creates additional karma where it did not previously exist. Again, this is not good or bad, right or wrong. It is purely a facet of karma. The abortion decision is seldom, if ever, made lightly, and there are those occasions where a desperate mother stops a child from entering a horrific situation. Judging a woman's decision to have an abortion denies the elements of karma that will accrue: both beneficial and detrimental.

If you stop a soul from entering what you perceive to be a terrible situation, is this good karma or bad karma? This is impossibly hard and is not for us to judge. In this situation, the energy of that *intention to protect a child from a horrible situation* is a mitigating factor in the karmic load for that mother and child, and all other parties present in this situation. Women do not experience abortion alone: there are always *other players* in the scenario, *who are also accruing karma.*

By stopping a birth, a different karmic path is created. If a birth was ceased due to timing and convenience, then this woman, and all the players, will have to atone through acknowledging the action, seeking forgiveness from the child, and from God, for stopping the pregnancy. Eventually the parents will have to forgive themselves as they do other kind acts of atonement for children.

The operative word here is to *mitigate* the karma created by the abortion, through remorse, prayer, spiritual practice and good deeds. Many feel what they have done cannot be forgiven. All true spiritual teachings remind us that <u>we are always lovable and forgivable souls,</u> the experience of abortion can be forgiven, and the karma created can be worked out and/or mitigated. Accepting this compassionate view alone can begin to heal a woman who has experienced an abortion. Let no one sit in judgment of her actions.

Men who knowingly encourage a woman to abort a fetus incur karma as well. The karmic load does not only attach to the mother. The father will also have to atone for the situation by acknowledging his role in the abortion, performing good deeds, and asking forgiveness of the fetus and of God.

Families who emotionally drive a woman to abort her child are also held karmically accountable. This, however, is never cut and dry, or black and white. There are so many factors that are involved in the denial of that incarnation, that only the Great Ones who balance the karmic scales can sort this out. Again, this is why one cannot judge abortion with a "good" or "bad" view. Nothing in life is ever this simple.

The Astral and the Physical Bodies

We are now at the point in our discussion, where the soul, or *Clear Light* of consciousness enters the physical body. There is an interface between these two bodies, which forms the basis of the spiritual nature of all of us. This is the beginning of our *conscious self* or personality. Our *subconscious self* is that part of us that makes our eyes blink and our body function and is charged with keeping us healthy. Our *super-conscious* or our Higher Self is our direct connection to the divine. All of these spiritually energetic parts of us are now forming. This is the creation of our *etheric body*. Everything starts in the etheric body and then becomes manifest in our physical bodies. This is

94

where the karmic elements of who we are, how our bodies will function and what we will look like begins to be formed.

These etheric elements then begin to focus on creating our meridian system, which is the basic chakra interface between our physical and our etheric body. All healing and illness begins in our etheric body, the foundation of our mind/body/health connection. If the emotions or the consciousness of the person are hurt, enraged, depressed, etc., these emotions, by definition must manifest in the physical body. They are intimately connected in illness, and the healing of the etheric body that leads to the healing of the physical body. Trauma can also affect the new baby including accidents or physical traumas caused by the mother or the father.

Reincarnating from Hell

There are those life streams that seem to be born vicious and even murderous. We have all met souls who may not be murderers but who may be mean, angry, and rage-filled despite a positive upbringing. Is it nature or nurture, the psychologists ask? Perhaps it is neither. What if a soul reincarnates from the darkest places in the 4th dimension or what is more commonly referred to as "hell?"

Frequently, a life stream or soul who is selfish, vicious, cruel and even murderous in one life becomes so hardened and focused on his evil mindset that this mental frequency of darkness becomes a dominant part of the person's Akashic record or soul memory. This record of all of his deeds and the dark part of his personality begins to wholly describe his soul. Murderers would not be expected to seek the light when death comes to them, and many times that soul will be in so much darkness that it would be hard for them to find the light, if it came. This is an example of souls who are not in an evolving process.

Current-day murderers do reincarnate from hell. These souls are born with a particular darkness in their souls that no amount of sweet-natured nurturing can erase. When the person is reborn, there are different family types the soul may experience. The person may be birthed into a family of similar lower or even a slightly higher frequency. Some families try to help these souls to take a different path while some families fuel the person's deadly tendencies. Many a family member has stood in stunned disbelief at the murderous actions of a son or daughter, sibling or parent. No one else in that family may be a murderer so they are left in sorrowful bewilderment at the actions of someone they have loved. Other families may further the soul's decline with more cruelty and abuse. The soul may also be abandoned at birth.

The reality is that life after life of shredded ethics, absent moral and spiritual values and a selfish desire to take advantage of others creates the formation of the criminal mind, making the person ripe for puppeting by a being from the Lower Astral or 4th dimension. Sometimes family members can stop them, but mostly they cannot.

In other words, if the soul is so consumed with him/herself and makes no progress towards positive soul evolution in each life span, then he or she must reincarnate with that vibration until their vibration can be raised. Families of serial killers often noted that their child began abusing insects and animals at a very early age. Their singular lack of conscience defined them from childhood. We see this today when children as young as seven and eight years of age, both male and female can murder with no conscience whatsoever.

This lack of moral compass defines the soul at a core level, which is why these types of souls do not reincarnate from the Heaven World, but from the Lower Astral. The theory basis is that malicious souls who do not cross over into the

Heaven World become residents of the Lower Astral and then reincarnate from there. If this is true, it would explain why so many of these souls start out as character disorders at the mild end (have you noticed the unnerving number of narcissists out there?) to cruel, heartless paranoid schizophrenics at the most dangerous end. These souls never had the benefit of the healing, guidance and wisdom of the Heaven World. All they received was a choking dose of darkness from the dens of hell.

This bleak outlook for souls reincarnating from the lower astral may not be totally hopeless. It is possible for a hardened soul from a previous life to become a better person in a future life *even if they did not reincarnate from the Heaven World.* Anything is possible.

This means that the love and energy that family members give to their criminally minded loved ones is not wasted energy. It is a critical step in the karmic path of the soul. It offers this darkened soul the opportunity to see a better way. Free will is the golden ticket to soul evolution. If the soul chooses a higher road, then life will improve. This is why some people feel that their life never works. This is also an aspect of karma. If you treated others badly in one life, then you must keep coming back until you learn to offer loving kindness to all beings.

Crossing over every single soul at death affords even the most hardened killer the opportunity for soul healing in the Heaven World. Souls do not have to remain in the hells. Crossing over a murderer, or any type of criminal at that person's death offers them a tremendous step up in his or her path to soul evolution. Crossing over murderous souls is tremendous service to the living, the dead and the souls who will encounter this former criminal in a future life. Perhaps in the next incarnation, this soul will not kill or harm anyone. Perhaps he or she will take more positive steps on their path *because they received that precious divine guidance from the Heaven World.*

What Did You Learn?

Native Americans have a profound understanding of reincarnation, so much so, that they do not refer to themselves as a soul, but as part of their body. They say, "my body is hungry," "my body is tired," not "I'm hungry, or I'm tired."

The ability to separate the concept of the physical body from the spiritual body was as completely natural to Native Americans as it is to many other religions in the world. It is ironically only the Judeo/Christian beliefs that have caused us to see the soul and body as one being _ which they are not. Once this concept is separated, then we can have a different view of how we live our lives.

It can also be helpful to understand that sometimes the karma for a situation is over. You are fired, lose your job, leave your home, get promoted or retire from a job. The karma for your time at that job is over, even if you can't see it at the time. This can be true for a marriage, a relationship or even a life. Each karmic experience has a time limit on it: an end date that means that it is time to evaluate what was learned, even after death.

If you find yourself grieving the end of an experience, the end of that particular karmic moment, no matter how long it has been, this is normal. Sometimes that grief is because it was so arduous and cruel or it can be because the event was amazingly precious and sweet. It is possible that someone's soul purpose was simply to survive or embrace the experience with heightened knowledge, wisdom and insight.

If we were to step back from our lives a bit and consider that each experience, no matter how challenging, is filled with karmic lessons, and if we could embrace those lessons, imagine our spiritual progress. Perhaps this concept could help us to take the sting out of betrayal, the heartbreak out of abandonment and grief, and the rage out of injustice.

What did you learn from each of those experiences?

Creating Future Incarnations - We Choose

Each person has the free will in each life to create a better life for themselves and for others. This is creating good karma. Creating good karma in turn directly and profoundly affects our future reincarnations. We absolutely create our futures now and for eternity. This is also why raising vibration is extremely important (see *Karma and Frequency*). The more you care for the physical body and your physical surroundings in each incarnation, the better body and better life you will have in the future, because you will have created a higher vibrational physical structure. This higher vibration *cannot* be placed in a physical body that is of a very low vibration – the physics, meaning the harmonic resonance simply would not match. The body would die.

As each of us progresses, hopefully we grow beyond where we were in that previous life. The more service we perform, the more we love and share that love, the more sophisticated and higher frequency our body becomes. In a practical sense, we will move from focusing on the lower, more base senses that drive human beings, to the loftier levels of spiritual evolution. We can become the ones who light the way for others by our humble service. Imagine if we could learn the lessons from challenging experiences and take a higher and higher road each lifetime. We are given the opportunity to heal our emotional wounds, our chronic sorrows and rise to greater and greater heights of happiness, love and, above all, wisdom.

Embracing the concepts of reincarnation has the potential to enable us all to do one particularly amazing thing: *live our lives knowing that we are going to have to return and be with all of these people again, and go through these experiences again, if we do not learn the critical lessons currently being presented.* Reincarnation is the gift the Father provides us to facilitate the path to soul evolution. Once we have advanced past the level of completing a variety of soul missions, we stop reincarnating because that part of our soul evolution will be at an end. Yes, there does come a moment in our cosmic history where reincarnating on Earth ceases.

The final irony is that most souls who reach this exalted level feel so much love and compassion for mortal people that they are filled with a bittersweet feeling. As much as they may be thrilled to be graduating to higher spiritual levels, at the same time they will desperately miss all those souls who offered them the experiences that spanned all of the lives they lived. Their saving grace will be that one day they too, will get to welcome those evolving souls to this new higher level.

Soul Mates and Love Mates

We have loved each other for centuries. Parents have adored children who died. Lovers have lost one another and grieved. Some of us remember those we have loved going back to Atlantis. Memory does not die with us. Memory is eternal: memory and love are the only two things we take with us at death. Those souls whose love transcends time and space are called soul mates or love mates. But these are not always romantic connections. Sometimes that parent-child connection is so tremendous that you can recognize your children from almost any past life, if you are sensitive to the possibility. Consider the following case.

I love Bath! This place is so gorgeous. My husband and I are so thrilled to be in this magical city. While visiting our daughter who lives here, we made a visit to the Abbey, the main church in the center of the town. It was beautiful inside. Alongside the walls and on the floor were the tombs of the people who had lived and died there for over 1300 years. I was reading the inscription on one of the tombs about an aunt whose heart was broken because her beloved niece died in her twenties. The words were so poignant and the woman's grief so raw that it evoked in me quite a bit of emotion. I read many of the inscriptions in that church, but none triggered that level of sadness. And it didn't leave me. I went back again and put my hand on the inscription. I began to cry inside. I had to leave the church. I realized that I was that aunt and the niece all those hundreds of years ago is my current daughter. Love transcends time; the years fell away and I could see myself standing by that tomb touching the words, tears streaming down my face. I could feel that grief as if it had happened yesterday. She and I are ancient soul mates. I am so grateful to have another life with her.

How do you know if someone is a *soul mate* or a *love mate*? Perhaps that answer lies in the nature of the relationship in the past, and in the need for healing, growth, and new experiences in the present. A person can be a soul or a love mate and the relationship will not be smooth. This concept is not always about romance, but about working out difficulties, about each person's soul purpose. This can be between parents and children, among siblings, between friends, employers and finally spouses.

I remember thinking: "He's so familiar. It's like I've always known him. Is this love at first sight? I wasn't sure that was real, but here it is, right in front of me. I feel as if I am already married to him, it's all coming back in a rush. I know him." And I did know him. Eventually I remembered that he is my soul mate and my love mate. This is the life that our soul purpose is to have a complete life together. I realized that in the past, one of us always died. Now after 46 years, we have realized our soul purpose. It's been tremendous.

The aspect of romance in finding a love mate has more to do with how you love yourself, your feelings regarding procreation and your need to grow, and of course, your karmic path is ever the constant. Some people never find love.

I would love to be married, but the hurt is so great, the pain of my horrible childhood is always there, like a cruel shadow self. I don't think I can give myself to a man. Oh, the loneliness. I want a relationship but the toxic relationship I had with my father has soured within me the idea of ever being with a man. Was my father my soul mate?

Yes, even an abusive father can be a soul mate. His soul purpose may have been *not to abuse his daughter.* Her soul purpose with him may have been to offer him the opportunity *not to abuse her.* He chose poorly. She feels forever damaged. When he failed his soul purpose his time, she may have found that her soul purpose may have also changed to simply learning how to heal herself from his abuse and work towards feeling like a normal woman.

Some people look for love in all the wrong faces, and some people find a loving and enduring union for decades. We all have multiple soul mates and they are usually our family members and closest friends. Some people disappoint us and others delight us with their love, compassion and other wonderful character traits. There is no black and white or simple answer when it comes to soul or love mates. Learning to love, standing up for yourself, healing and growing emotionally and spiritually, are the main elements here.

Characters in the Play

Do all the characters in our lives return to play the same roles with us life after life? Yes and no. We reincarnate with the same souls repeatedly so that we help each other learn important lessons. Sometimes you are your mother's sister, or child, or spouse or in-law. It depends on what both of you need. Your sibling may not always be your sibling life after life, or your spouse, or boss. We play different roles so that we can walk in the shoes of all the characters in the play that make up our lives.

Some lives we will be male and some lives female. We may go centuries as the same sex for the full realm of that experience. We may be the same race for a very long time or perhaps just one or two lifetimes.

We drop into the drama of the religion of our parents and decide if that faith will be the best tool to take with us as we walk our spiritual path.

There are lots of clues to our past lives; look around and see them. What is of interest: the American West, Europe, Africa, the Roaring Twenties, World War II, the Civil War, Egypt? Perhaps a life was experienced in that location, in that era. And then there are those things that elicit passion within us: is it motherhood, food, crystals, engineering, music, math? A lifelong interest in medicine, law, the sea or another area may mean that there were many lifetimes spent in association with these topics.

Study the following list to begin to identify those clues:

- childhood games
- preferences
- cultures
- historical events
- talents & abilities
- books & films
- fears and phobias
- geographical

- clothing styles
- food preferences
- time periods
- occupations
- race & heritage
- personality traits
- art preferences
- déjà vu

- climates
- architecture
- body scars
- mannerisms
- animals & pets
- dreams
- locations
- familiar faces

How Do Past Lives Relate to Mental and Physical Illness?

Many times, specific mental and physical illnesses have their root cause in past lives. You are given life after life to work out these issues. Frequently, the issues are so difficult that the person may not approach working it out for dozens of lifetimes, unless there is more than just standard allopathic or traditional psychotherapy done for the person.

People with serious sexual dysfunction frequently were raped or, many times, were the rapist in past lives. This same person can be male or female in this life – it matters not. It is not necessary to know exactly what happened in that past life. Simply addressing the mental and physical situation from a spiritual view can frequently release the old pattern, and the person can move forward with their life.

Grief from a past life can have a direct influence on a current life. This can manifest in all types of *fear of* scenarios. Grief can create a sense of profound vulnerability within a soul, which manifests as *fear of* a wide variety of things. Perhaps a child died. This new parent may appear to be over protective, hovering, perhaps the modern "helicopter parent." If a spouse died, this grief can manifest as being afraid to commit to a relationship or being fearful that something could happen to a relationship. Healing this, or any type of grief, requires that the soul begin to understand that all life carries with it inherent risk. One of the risks of loving another human being is the risk that this person could leave, either voluntarily or through death. We love people. Sometimes they die or divorce us, but we must go on living, for that is the spiritual and karmic test being offered in each lifetime.

Many mental illnesses can be caused by other things on a psychic level, in addition to the trauma of past life experiences. Consider that all addictions like alcoholism and drug addiction are almost impossible to overcome. This is because alcohol and drugs, tobacco and gambling create holes in the person's auric field and open up doorways for dead alcoholics, gamblers, smokers and drug addicts to enter that person's physical body. Once these addicted ghosts attach to a living soul, they *push the soul to keep drinking or taking drugs or perpetuating the addiction.* Up to 60 different ghosts can inhabit a person at a time. It gets pretty crowded in there! This is why these heavily inhabited mortal people have no memory of what they did while under the influence of these toxic substances or behaviors. Could these types of addictions or habits be a holdover from a past life? Of course, they can be that and more. These types of addictions are very slow forms of suicide. The person numbs themselves to the challenges of everyday life due to a prior grief or sadness from this or a past life. The person continues to incur negative karma through all of this as well. Unless the soul steps up to the karmic plate and overcomes this addiction, this desire to escape the challenges of mortal life will keep returning.

What About Suicide?

It is very difficult to say with any certainty what happens to a soul in a current life if he or she committed suicide in a previous life. What happens between lives is a huge determining factor in how a person will live a future life. This is why it is absolutely critical that any soul who has committed suicide be afforded the comfort and rescue of **The Crossing Over Prayer** and The **Compassion Prayer for Suicide**. These and other prayers are also available at **GhostHelpers.com**. The purpose of these prayers is to facilitate the soul's crossing over into the Heaven World to finally receive the love and healing that only the 5th dimensional energies of this higher realm can provide.

Souls who languish in the 4th dimension reincarnate from the 4th dimension and their learning, healing and insight are often extremely limited coming from that toxic dimension, that extremely low, resonant harmonic frequency location.

It is difficult to say what a person desires in terms of experiences. Suicide is a last resort, a hopelessness resulting from profound grief, fear, self-loathing and prison-like depression. Hopefully someone may come into their lives to help them reconsider. The effort that people make to prevent suicide is of supreme importance. Suicide affects not only the specific soul, but also all the family members, friends, co-workers, and anyone whose life they have touched. Suicide also affects their karma and the karma of those who sought to prevent the death.

However, people who take their own life *very frequently never tell anyone how depressed they are or overtly ask for help.* Family members seeking answers and blaming themselves would be wise to consider these facts. Sometimes no one can appreciate the level of darkness and despair that their loved one or friend felt. Guilt will not help the grieving to heal.

Many people believe that souls are punished for committing suicide. The truth is that each soul's karma determines what happens to them after death and in the future. *Punished* has a variety of meanings. One person's punishment can easily be construed by another as simply another opportunity *not to commit suicide* when confronted with the same set of depressing circumstances.

The compassion of a loving God is without end. Forgiveness is inherent in the very nature of the Father, regardless of religion, belief system or having no belief and regardless of method of death. The harmonic frequency of someone who takes his or her own life is extremely low. It is in fact the lowest frequency, even lower than murder. Violence against oneself is a tremendous level of self-loathing and this soul will need all the Divine assistance he or she can find. Cross these souls over; afford them the light of the Divine and the hope of healing all those fractured, vulnerable parts of their souls. Imagine how this will help them in their future incarnations and the path of soul evolution.

What About Murder?

Are murderers and the people they murdered in a reincarnation pattern? Are they soul mates? Have all murder victims known their murderers in a past life?

Reincarnation is the only way we can come to understand that 75-80% of murder victims *know their murderers*. The real percentage is believed to be 100% because you may not *consciously know your murderer but there are pretty tremendous odds you have known this person from a past life*. This removes the random element to many acts of "senseless" violence, including multiple murders. Karma attaches to every single action and that karma is paid forward in a myriad of ways. In some cases, one soul or soul group offers another soul the opportunity *not to commit murder*. It may seem like there has to be a better way to manage this but this is how it currently works.

There are several factors in operation. The earlier discussions of soul *devolution* identified the fact that when a soul is abused, that part of that soul is *shaved off*. Eventually, over lifetimes, enough of that soul is removed that he or she no longer feels human, nor can this soul respond to normal human emotion. It is as if their resonant frequency, the level at which this soul is vibrating is abysmally low. These souls then become puppets of dark beings in the 4th dimension. In these cases, the puppeted soul is no longer exercising free will and kills at the will of the puppeteer in the 4th dimension. Yes, the killer still has free will, but as less and less of him or her is still there, there is a greatly diminished capacity to exercise free will or human consciousness, awareness of action and reaction: they simply don't care what they do to others.

This is the reason it is so critical to cross over every

possible murderer. Once in the Heaven World, the missing pieces of the soul can be restored so that in the next life, when he or she meets his murder victim soul mate, he can choose *not to kill him or her.* Now the karmic pattern will have been changed and life will be different for both of these souls. *Not killing may become the entire soul purpose for that reincarnated soul from the Heaven World.*

Karma and the Law of Reincarnation

Curses, the Evil Eye, Jinxes, Hexes, Spells and Wishes

Some people feel they were born cursed.

Others feel as if the evil eye were always upon them.

There are people who believe that some witch put a hex (the German term) or spell on them.

Are curses, evil eyes, jinxes, spells and hexes real? Can some sort of witch or magician put some magic spell on a soul as they reenter mortal life?

Fairy tales, the magic carpet of myth and legend tell us how witches, viziers, black magicians, evil kings and queens and dark beings work so hard to place a "spell" or curse on the hero or heroine in the epic tale. However, the lesson of these brutal, malicious and creative stories is that with pluck and daring, profound love and courage even the humblest man or woman can beat the odds and overcome evil. The hero of the story never dies.

Is this reality? Or is the truth somewhere in between myth and legend?

Karma is the truth. Karma never wastes energy and the effort that any person puts into overcoming what they perceive as a dark cloud over them will enable them to learn and grow. Sounds prosaic, simplistic doesn't it? If the epic hero in humble human form is "true of heart" then this person doesn't have the karma to be killed, stopped or defeated. He or she may have to work an entire lifetime to get to that point, suffer tremendous disappointment, sometimes defeat and great emotional pain – but along the way the karmic energy of this struggle will have unimagined benefits.

He struggled all of his life to find success. He felt he was under a terrible black cloud. All of his efforts seem to have been stolen. Nothing worked. But his wife never left his side. She was always there working hard to improve her already considerable psychic abilities to see if she could help on a higher spiritual level. In her effort to help her husband, she rose to higher and higher levels of spiritual ability and insight. She was tireless and relentless in her desire to help him. She never questioned that he had the karma for success so she kept up her quest to find that path that would help the light to shine on him. But he died before any of his efforts could bear fruit. When she looked back on his life, she could see that along the way, he was an inspiration to all the people whose lives he touched. He was adored on multiple levels. Despite his sadness, he never lost the element that made him revered: his true heart. His life may have appeared to be marginally successful by some but for her, he was a hero to many and a soul mate for her on every level. Because of him, she could do amazing things and he improved her ability to help others on much more sophisticated levels. When she crossed him over he had quite the reception committee of divine beings waiting for him for the true prince he was. He was her soul mission and in the final irony, perhaps she was his soul mission.

Heroes come in so many forms. Success has a variety of measurements and in the end, love and service do overcome the darkness of the thoughts and perceptions of ourselves, and others.

However, as we have discussed, if a person suffered horribly in previous lives and more and more bits and pieces of their soul were sheared off, then this person may feel as if they are "being puppeted" to have bad things happen to them or they feel "compelled" to do bad things to other people. There is no curse or hex spell or jinx. There is only the karma the soul has earned and is working through on their soul evolution path.

Do We Reincarnate as Animals?

There is a belief among some people that we frequently come back as animals. This is not necessarily a cheery thought. If you were a "snake in the grass" in this life, do you come back as a rattlesnake? Is this true? No, a soul is a soul and cannot ever come back as an animal: it is the nature of being a human soul.

It is also the concept of soul evolution. All things are evolving, from mountains to trees, bodies of water to bees. As each life form evolves it moves to different levels. Consider that hive insects, like bees, ants, and wasps have to learn how to work together for the common good. We speak about the food chain but what is more visible is the evolutionary chain of development of all creatures. Who is high on the evolutionary chain? Elephants have an entire family matriarchy, rules and even death rituals. Elephants grieve their fellow family members and have a tremendous memory for people, places and things. This is true for whales, dolphins and orcas. These creatures feel what is happening. They are obviously at a much higher level than mere fish. Perhaps creatures evolve past being in a school of a fish to being larger and larger fish until they graduate to being mammals. What comes after being a great whale or a dolphin? Perhaps some of them spiritually leave the water and evolve into the lesser apes until they arrive at the level of the great apes. These creatures have entire family societies, lovingly caring for their young.

In the canine world, some of the top dogs are the ones are in a position to help their human owners through difficult times. Some of the most superior ones are the guide dogs and the working dogs for the military, law enforcement and drug interdiction. Some dogs sniff out bombs and in some countries are honored with a funeral with full military honors at death.

The exact path is shrouded in mystery but soul evolution has to begin somewhere; there has to be a first step. However, human beings are never animals. Human souls are in a class by themselves.

Beware the Egocentric Psychic

What if you and a friend decide to visit a psychic and all of a sudden the psychic decides to tell you or your spouse about *what he or she perceives to have been one of your past lives or your past life together.* Stop her in her tracks! *Never allow someone to tell you about one of your past lives.* Many egocentric or perhaps well-intentioned psychics are eager to tell you or anyone else about their perceptions of one of your past lives. *The problem is that you have no way of proving what he or she is telling you is true.* What's more, this sharing of questionable knowledge can definitely influence your perception of yourself and possibly other family members and friends. It may also influence your future and change the course of your karmic path.

There is a karmic factor here.

112

It is a violation of spiritual law to tell someone his or her past lives.

Telling someone who you think he or she was, or what this person may have done in a past life, violates spiritual law because it effectively robs the person of discovering the information for him or herself. It directly interferes with that person's karmic path. This is critical because the person who believes he or she knows what happened could be completely mistaken. Now the erroneous information may impact the person in such a manner that they cannot see themselves the same way and may take regrettable action because of false information. This can create stumbling blocks on the path of the person sharing the information, as well as the recipient of the information.

The psychic earns negative karma for violating this spiritual tenet and the recipient of the information earns questionable karma for hearing it and responding to it in any manner. It is virtually impossible *not to respond* to the news of who or what someone thinks you were in a past life. However, if you are able to stop them from blurting out their opinion, then this karma can be forestalled for all the parties.

Let us examine the ripple effect of looking at this. One of the most frequent things psychics tell someone is that he or she was "a healer from Atlantis" in that previous incarnation. This is problematic because now the person's ego has been fed. They now believe they can heal. However, without properly studying *how to heal, and the precautions to take to care for your own body, the person can unwittingly take on the illness of the person he or she thinks they are healing.* Some amateur healers actually unintentionally rob their subjects of their own energy and do not give them any healing at all. This false/questionable information can create illness in both the supposed healer and the person seeking healing.

One psychic, albeit well-intentioned, told her client

that she was either an Initiate or a great master in another life. The psychic also told her that she, the client, was *so advanced* that her very being here on Earth was positively influencing the planet, and that things she *must do in the future* would actually influence the tectonic plates of the earth, and oh by the way, she was also a great healer from Atlantis.

But the reality was much different. In this incarnation, the client's life was a mess: she had a terrible relationship with her husband, challenges with other friends and family members, and now she has a greatly heightened sense of self-importance. *This woman absolutely believed the psychic because she wanted it to be real.* She believed that this one dubious story, completely unverifiable opinion from one person was unquestionably true. One encounter with this psychic caused this woman to believe that she was spiritually responsible for changes on planet Earth. She became completely carried away with her perceived self-importance. The psychic's comment had unintended consequences. No one could reason with this client or even gingerly question whether or not this could be true. She became incensed, believing to her core that she had to take care of the Earth's tectonic plates and that she was a great healer.

When questioned about how she planned to manage these tectonic plates, she huffed smugly that she would "just know." One can only hope that she did not harm herself or others in the process.

Another man was told that he was a *very advanced* healer in Atlantis. He spent thousands of dollars going to this creative psychic to learn more and more questionable information about this supposed past life on that doomed continent. All the while, his own health began to go downhill.

Still another woman was told that she was a goddess and performed acts as a high priestess for a certain group from a past life in Atlantis. The receiver of the information never once questioned what this might actually mean. *She wanted to believe it.*

How does any psychic know if anything they think they are seeing is true? They cannot possibly know that. Even if they suspect that they could be right, *it does not give them the right to deprive the individual in front of them of their own private exploration of their past lives.* Telling someone his or her past life is a serious violation of spiritual law because it interferes with that person/soul's free will and that person's soul evolution. Unfortunate karma is created in these instances.

Some psychics will argue that they *feel compelled* to tell the person what they think they are seeing about that person's past life. Spiritual discipline, and the laws of karma, dictate that no words be mentioned or offered. Where is the compulsion to tell this information coming from: ego, genuine care or a false sense of importance?

If a psychic has said something to you about what your past life could have been, take the information lightly and go on with your day. It is probably not true. The most important moment that should glean your powerful attention is the present moment and the spiritual service you are making. Focus on your soul evolution, not the ego trip someone has purchased for you.

Not Interested in Past Lives?

What if you do not want to face your actions from a previous life or have no interest in past lives?

No one says you have to explore past lives, nor is it necessary. Live the best, most productive life you possibly can. If someone makes you feel uncomfortable, vow to forgive them, and yourself, for whatever happened in the past, and to make a new beginning – to be a different person, and to change past patterns. These actions alone can make wonderful changes for you and those around you.

You frequently see some conflict over this between couples. One spouse will be fascinated by the whole concept of past lives, and the other will feign no interest. Both opinions are valid, important, and should not be judged. What is good for one person is not necessarily beneficial for another. Spouses need to be respectful of each other's preferences.

The Lessons of the Masters: We Are Immortal

Life Everlasting: Soul Evolution in Karmic Time

Reincarnation is the concept that we live forever, that we return to God, and that we are reborn again and again to experience spiritual growth. If we believe that God is just, and that the Divine does exist, then we must also look at Christ's concepts of *life everlasting* as a reality.

We know that Christ referred to life everlasting. Perhaps we have all wondered how much time is "everlasting." Is the concept of everlasting, another way to speak of karmic time? Is the process of achieving the awareness of a karmic lesson the meaning of being in the karmic moment?

If life everlasting is true, then the reality is that we return life after life after life after life for a seeming eternity of soul evolution opportunities. Sometimes we live short lives, perhaps only a few days. In other lives, we live longer, perhaps over 100 years.

Each life will present us with special events, stunning turning points where we must make a karmic choice. We say that this is that soul's "karmic moment." Sometimes it means that a soul must make a choice in which direction he or she will go. Sometimes these are moments when our ethics are tested; perhaps we will be morally tempted to keep a vow and do the right thing, remember our commitment or show tremendous courage. Karma gives us "do-overs" so that we can test ourselves to make sure that we have passed the karmic tests.

Some tests are severe. These are the tests where one person may sacrifice his or her life for another. Some decisions carry with them a crushing weight of consequence: a profound karmic moment. Every single test offers the soul the chance to:

- Do the right thing even when it is very hard.
- Speak the truth, even if it means that someone will be angry with us.
- Listen to that still small voice that warns us of danger.
- Step up with courage to a challenging task, risking the possibility of failure.
- Leave a toxic situation when there is no visible hope it will change.
- Stop creating terrible karma for someone by stepping away from him or her when they are abusing you. Yes, if you allow continued abuse, you automatically incur negative karma for yourself because you did not put a stop to it.
- Awaken to the possibility that you can leave a situation forever and free yourself and possibly your children as well.

The list of karmic moments is endless. Be mindful when yours is facing you and act with the highest moral, ethical and spiritual courage. Consider the following examples:

A young man is faced with continuing to live with a

chronically abusive family. He resists the unrelenting abuse of his father and fights back. Finally, his father throws him out, telling him not to come back. This is a critical karmic moment: he can either beg to return to the abuse or make a clean break with the abuse that may have been going on for lifetimes. He has several choices facing him. Every choice carries with it karma of some kind. Finally, after being with several families, he finds a family that "feels like he is home." He is stunned. He begins a very different life. His journey is not easy. He has to adjust to a radically different paradigm, a better one, a higher frequency life. Some days are tough going but he sticks it out and his entire life path changes. Everyone helps him. People begin to see his goodness, his intelligence and his potential. As the years pass he becomes a man that his wife, children and adoptive family not only love but admire. He saw his karmic moment and embraced it.

A young mother discovers that her six-year-old daughter is incredibly psychic. In fact, her psychic ability seems to grow daily including the ability to see ghosts, remote view various locations, have medical intuition, and hear the thoughts of animals. Her daughter is unnervingly accurate. But there are dark elements that accompany psychic ability and this mom is desperate to try to find help with this unorthodox situation. After 18 months of searching out and meeting all types of psychics, she finally encounters a mentor. She discovers that she needs this woman on an ongoing basis because so much is happening every day with her daughter – but she cannot pay her. Now the karmic moment arrives for the mom and the psychic. This intuitive recognizes that this mom is going to require guidance for quite a while and she offers a trade of services. The psychic needs an editor – would the mom be willing to help out here? The partnership that ensued not only helped the very young precocious psychic but also the far more wise and insightful "senior" psychic. The mom finally found the help she needed and discovered along the way not only how to help her own daughter, but the children of her friends who were also psychic. Many bountiful blessings came from all parties recognizing that karmic moment.

What about the karmic moments where ethics are critical? How about those whistleblowers that try to warn us of the dangers that they see? One man warned the American public about the government spying on American citizens – without a warrant. Several scientists from various government agencies have bravely stood up and warned us about the dangers of genetic modifications to the food and medical supply. Some have suffered terribly but the karma of their positive intentions will eventually stand them in good stead.

Once you have faced the many karmic moments that present themselves to you throughout your life, then you will begin to see how your very soul is evolving into a far more wise, patient and benevolent spiritual being/evolving soul.

Then that day comes when you stop reincarnating on this planet and move on to higher spiritual realms for a greater expansion of your soul evolution. Perhaps this is the best definition of reincarnation: soul evolution.

Christ's generous statement of life everlasting is the everlasting karmic opportunity to live every lifetime to the fullest.

The fact that in roughly 75 years the world population has gone from 1.6 billion to 7.4 billion is staggering. This can only mean that there are an astounding number of souls who must have very specific experience requirements as we enter the new millennia. The birth rate may appear to be at an all-time high. At the same time, we are seeing the increasing number of natural and manmade disasters. Yet many countries are seeing their birth rates drop: some countries are no longer replacing themselves. So, it is possible that the global population is beginning to level out and reduce itself.

Souls may also have to be scheduled to take advantage of certain global situations so that karma can be balanced. This may be why death rates from cancers and other illnesses are as high as they are. People may be dying and returning at an accelerating rate, simply to get in all the experiences necessary to advance enough to embrace the coming new age.

Centuries in the past, people lived and died very quickly, having dull, often extremely mundane experiences. Soul evolution progress was slow at best, because life and culture in those past times was essentially the same over hundreds of years, so significant progress was hard to acquire. Because there is so much to learn now, there is a feeling that time is accelerating and that people are returning/reincarnating with brief times between death.

We Are Immortal

We are all immortal.

We are created to have an equal opportunity to grow and develop spiritually.

We are all subject to the laws of karma. *No one is exempt.*

We are not *created equal.* We are all created uniquely *because of the karma we have each generated in our past lives.* This uniqueness, this karmic signature, resonant frequency or vibration, is what defines us and determines where we are on the soul evolutionary ladder.

The earth is a schoolhouse of mortal experiences to help our immortal soul advance on its path of soul evolution. *If this concept can live within each of us, then it means that we can live with more insight and hope, more responsibility and caring.*

Soul evolution is not found in endlessly seeking psychics to tell our futures by flipping mysteriously decorated cards.

We do not grow spiritually by playing Ouija or violent video games that have us enslaved to some artificially created master who can infiltrate our dreams and influence our lives.

We cannot understand God by going to séances to contact the dead souls languishing for eternity in the 4th dimension.

Channeling some dark intelligence without due diligence will never contribute to our soul evolution in any positive way.

Believing that you are born in sin and that you will die in sin is one of the most significant inhibitors of soul evolution ever invented by a supposed Christian religion.
Christ never said this.

A mortal person said this and now millions of souls are labeled as *sinners,* endlessly admonished to confess and/or repent. The guilt this alone engenders is staggering and dramatically lowers that person's resonant frequency. It causes them to feel unworthy at the point of death, believing that God could never love or welcome them home to the Heaven World. This is untrue, cruel and heartless.

Believing that following men in long, black outfits, who call themselves *men of the cloth,* is the way to find God negates the individual responsibility all souls have, the priesthood of all believers, to seek God in their own way and on their own terms. We have the right to follow our individual spiritual journeys without the interference, questionable influence or dark cloak of guilt provided by these men.

How can someone truly be on the path to spiritual enlightenment when he or she allows prescription drugs, illegal drugs (including marijuana) or alcohol, to take over their minds and bodies?

Only souls who take total responsibility for their own

spiritual path find that soul evolution is real to them. It is important to their progress to seek to *know God in all ways.*

Is it acceptable to make money in a business setting with an underlying spiritual basis? In today's society, how will we know if we are doing that, meaning focusing on our business spiritual basis, unless we consciously seek this karmic answer? No one doubts that companies have to make money, but some companies, whether it is in the health care field, industry, education, or aviation as an example, use their positions to ruthlessly take advantage of the very customers they should be honoring. Ironically, it feels as if the larger the company is, the greater the distance becomes between the CEO and the 'C' suite, and the users who fuel their business.

I wonder if the boys upstairs, the owners of this stupid airline have any idea what a nightmare they have created for their passengers by now charging for luggage? How cruel is that? It's become a nightmare for we flight attendants who somehow have to help people juggle their gigantic carry on and the tiny bins we have for them. People feel cheated. I get it. So do I.

Sometimes it's a game to see how much money can be made without regard to the consequences for the end user.

How much money is enough for them? How can they take such ruthless advantage of people with electric rates this high? People are suffering don't they care? Who are these people? Who is Enron???

Being on a spiritual path is critical in understanding that business, balanced with a wise eye, can benefit the person giving and the person receiving. This concept is a huge step, either forward or backward, on the part of all parties on their soul evolution path.

Wealth is not evil if it is balanced with a view to the karmic ramifications of managing it on an emotional/spiritual level. This means that it is important to be aware of how wealth is earned and shared, when it is appropriate. The important point is how a person operates in business can either positively or negatively affect the evolution of their soul, depending on whether it is in support of the higher good of others, or not in support of the higher good of others, regardless of whether there is financial gain from the business or not.

By the same token, people who are invited to work hard and grow, but want it all given to them, earn an equally challenging karma as do the super wealthy who sometimes mistreat or turn a blind eye to those less fortunate than themselves. However, all of these things constitute freedom-of-choice experiences that can regress our spiritual progress or advance it.

We Are All Old Souls

We have discussed the roles of karma and energy, frequency and vibration. Understanding the role of energy in past lives is a natural follow on to this thought progression. Here is the logic trail:

- If energy is neither created nor destroyed, then the energy that animates us – that part of us that is our soul – lives forever.

- If we are here for experiences, then the soul needs many lifetimes of experiences to grow to ever-expanding levels of enlightenment. At the end of each lifespan, the energy of each soul must return somewhere.

- If energy spent is never wasted, then the energy you spent learning a lesson in one lifetime may give you the wisdom to be of much greater service and gain more intense insight in the next lifetime.

- The karma you create in one lifetime may come full circle and manifest in another lifetime be it positive or negative. It is not always possible to expend all of your karma in one lifetime because the power of the experiences would be too intense, so karma may be spread over many lifetimes.

- The power of your intuitive ability may grow ever stronger as you learn how to operate in more than one dimension.
- As you use your psychic ability to learn and grow you may find that you learn to love humanity with a deep and abiding passion.
- You will see others not so much as the same as yourself but as unique souls on a path of advancement.
- When this knowledge sweeps over you, compassion begins to live within you and your frequency will automatically rise to greater levels of divine connection.

How many times have you heard someone look at another person, nod knowingly, and say: "She's an old soul." The truth is the energy of the soul continues to operate for eternity: *we are all old souls.* So a past life is one of the many thousands of experiential endeavors we have had in the learning process that is soul evolution. It is like going to school: you are not finished learning simply because you finish a grade.

Be the Evolving Soul

When we can each look in the mirror and see an evolving soul instead of a person with human failings, instead of a flawed individual, we will begin to make mighty strides on our spiritual path of soul evolution. It also means that we can *recognize that we have a path to follow and that we alone are in charge of walking that path.*

Walking the path back to the divine means that we no longer hope that God is on our side. We seek to *know God in all ways and always.* We awaken one day to an awareness that we seek to be on God's side, to do his work in our own humble way, a way of service to humanity.

Embracing the concept that we will eventually make a final return to the Heaven World once we have earned that level of elevated karma, evolved and progressed, enables us to see a path beyond this moment, and truly understand that we will all end up among the stars as lights for eternity.

About the Authors

Tina Erwin CDR USN (Ret) has studied metaphysics for many years, gaining insight into the interpersonal relationships at the heart of everyday living. Her writing comes from an intense desire to know and understand the unseen world of action and reaction, combined with a sincere desire to share this understanding with other knowledge seekers. Her first book, The *Lightworker's Guide to Healing Grief*, is a treatise on how to help yourself or someone else to heal grief. Her second book, *The Lightworker's Guide to Everyday Karma*, is a lighthearted look at applying the principles of karmic law to everyday life.

Her third, fourth and fifth books, *Ghost Stories from the Ghost's Point of View Trilogy, Volumes 1, 2 and 3*, introduce what it is like to be dead, what it is like to discover that the life you thought you were going to have is never going to happen. Literally you see the ghosts' point of view.

Her lifelong studies into the deeper meaning of events and actions were further enhanced by the experiences of a dynamic, 20-year career in the Navy, working for the U.S. Submarine Force, retiring at the Commander level.

Commander Erwin found the Navy to be a tremendous schoolhouse in which to study all the facets of behavior, from the worst to the finest levels of humanity.

Tina lives in San Diego, CA. She has been happily married to the love of her life, submariner, CDR Troy Erwin, USN (Ret), for over 40 years. She holds a Bachelor of Science in Industrial Relations and a Masters in Management.

She has an extensive collection of videos, which can be found both on YouTube and on her website: www.TinaErwin.com.

You can learn more about her books, podcast and her videos on her website: www.TinaErwin.com or connect with her: Tina@TinaErwin.com.

Be sure to listen to her podcast: The Karmic Path co-hosted with Laura Van Tyne at **https://TheKarmicPath.com/**. Have questions on karma, contact her at: **Questions@TheKarmicPath.com**.

Laura Van Tyne started out as a "normal" person. She was an educator, with a Master's Degree in Education, working as a schoolteacher in the San Diego School system. She was also married with three active daughters. She volunteered within her community. Her husband was a businessman who would coach soccer on the weekends for their daughters' teams. Pretty normal stuff: until one day everything changed.

What happens when you wake up and you find your child to be exceptionally psychic? How does this affect your child, and your family? How does raising a psychic child change how you parent? Laura discovered that there were no parenting books on how to raise a psychic child, much less any explanation of what the ramifications were of the misuse of that ability. When Laura's youngest child was 5 years old, she could see and hear things that her parents could not. Laura felt blind and helpless: how could she protect her daughter against things that she could not see or hear? How would Laura truly know if whatever, or whoever, was talking to her youngest daughter, was there for her higher good? Laura would not let her run out into the street by herself to see the ice cream truck – why on earth would she want her talking to ghostly strangers? What is the karma in all of this?

Laura's questions and concerns forced her to educate herself to find some way to take her power back. In the process, she learned what worked and what didn't. When she and Tina Erwin finally made that fateful connection, both of their lives changed.

Learn more about Laura's story on her website: LauraVanTyne.com or contact her at **Laura@LauraVanTyne.com**.

Be sure to listen to her podcast: The Karmic Path co-hosted with Tina Erwin at **https://TheKarmicPath.com/** Have questions on karma, contact her at: **Questions@TheKarmicPath.com**

57016128R00086

Made in the USA
Middletown, DE
26 July 2019